Complete recordings of four charts and many examples of jazz styles,
solo singing techniques, and concert choir/jazz choir sound comparisons.

THE COMPLETE GUIDE
TO TEACHING

VOCAL JAZZ

(Including Pop and Other Show Styles)

BY

DR. STEPHEN ZEGREE

30/1737H
ISBN: 0-89328-153-0
Distributed by The Lorenz Corporation
P.O. Box 802
Dayton, Ohio 45401-0802

Table of Contents

CD Track List

Acknowledgements

Writing a book is by no means a solitary project. I am grateful to so many people who were involved in the creation of this book that it is difficult to know where to begin. First, to all of my former, current and future students and members of the Gold Company program at Western Michigan University, my heartfelt thanks for teaching me at least as much as I have taught you. I hope that I have had a positive effect on your musical, professional, and personal lives as much as my primary teachers, including Dr. Eph Ehly, Dr. Paul Aliapoulios, David Baker, David Bean, and Richard Cass, have influenced me.

My heartfelt thanks to my friends Phil Mattson, Frank De Miero and Kirby Shaw who were foolish enough to take me under their wings when I was a "young pup" and vocal jazz novice and offer me guidance and inspiration.

Also, many thanks to my friends in the vocal groups that continue to inspire me through their recordings, live performances, and high standards of musical excellence — The Manhattan Transfer and Janis Siegel, New York Voices and Darmon Meader, Take Six and Doctor(!) Cedric Dent, The Real Group, The Hi-Lo's and The Singers Unlimited (you gotta love Don and Bonnie!). Special thanks to my friend Bobby McFerrin who has shown the world the limitless possibilities of the human voice and enabled all of us to take chances and have fun.

Thank you to my friends Gene Puerling, Clare Fischer, Ward Swingle, Michele Weir and Gary Fry, all wonderful composers and arrangers, who have generously given so much of themselves in the interest of setting standards and creating beautiful music.

To Sally Russell, Emily Crocker and Lynn Sengstack: thank you for giving me the opportunity to publish vocal jazz arrangements that apparently have given many people an equal dose of pleasure and frustration over the years. Special thanks also go to Shawnee Press for giving us permission to use excerpts from two of their publications, *But Beautiful* (#A-1991) and *This Masquerade* (#A-2101). The two other pieces used as musical examples (*Doctor Blues* [#15/1744H] and *One In A Million*[#15/1743H]) are published by Heritage Music Press.

Thank you to my wonderful friends and colleagues at Western Michigan University who make the prospect of "going to work" something that I honestly look forward to, and from whom I continue to learn: Diana Spradling, Sunny Wilkinson, Trent Kynaston, Tom Knific, Tim Froncek, Billy Hart, John Campos, Rick O'Hearn, Dr. Joe Miller, Joan Bynum, Gail Otis Birch, Mark J. Evert, Carl Doubleday and Margaret Hamilton.

Specifically, thanks to the following people for reading sections of the book and offering invaluable feedback: Diana Spradling (my conscience who continually keeps me in line) for reading and offering tremendous insights and suggestions, and for offering the wonderful forms on selecting repertoire and listening to music. Sunny Wilkinson for her input on solo singing, writing a lead sheet, and for her superb solo singing demonstration on the **CD**. Tom Knific and Tim Froncek for their input on bass, guitar and drum set playing. Nancy Bocek, the terrific choreographer. I would not have *dared* to include a chapter on choreography without her stamp of approval! John Jacobson for his friendship and invaluable inspiration on choreography and staging.

Thanks also go to Jeff Chaffin for his support and advice on all things technical and especially for his guidance on the **PA** system chapter. My graduate assistant Justin Binek for terrific research and assistance in the assembly of the discography. The incomparable Jed Scott for helping make the studio recording sessions, mixing and production one less thing I had to worry about. To Cathy Pfeiler-Bielawski, Susan Rice, Sarah Walker and Ted Richards, our high school choral director "readers" who helped with each revision and kept me from straying too far into left field or standing on too many soap boxes.

My sincerest thanks also go to the people at Lorenz — Geoff Lorenz and Larry Pugh supported the project throughout, Gregg Sewell took all of the electronic files and made them look like a book, and the ebullient and effervescent Mary Lynn Light-foot had many words of encouragement along the way. Also at Lorenz, my thanks go to Blair Bielawski (a.k.a. Peter Blair) for encouraging me to undertake this entire project ("Curse you..."), and for his tireless efforts, encouragement, edits, suggestions, help keeping me on task and on time, and his general good humor.

I'd also like to acknowledge the terrific JazzWorks Big Band for their enthusiastic and swinging playing on our demonstration **CD**. It's always a kick for Gold Company to sing with a big band! Speaking of Gold Company, they also have earned my heartfelt thanks. Their contribution to our demo **CD** was invaluable. They continue to inspire and impress me with their talent and their dedication to music.

Thanks also go to my "brother" Duane Davis, for his support and involvement in the Gold Company program, and for agreeing to direct Gold Company for a year, allowing me a sabbatical and the desperately needed time to complete this project.

To my friend and *great* operatic baritone Tim Noble, thanks for teaching me that singers *can* read music *and* count, and that opera singers can also sing in the jazz and pop style with equal success.

Finally to my family, my mother and sister, whose suggestions and input were most helpful, to the memory of my father (I truly think he would be proud of this book, even though I didn't become a lawyer) and to my daughter Sarah and son Nathaniel for teaching me wisdom and patience, and bringing more joy into my life than you will ever know! I love you all.

Dr. Stephen Zegree
Kalamazoo, Michigan
October 2001

Forewords

A master teacher/conductor/musician, Dr. Steve Zegree shares some of the philosophies, methodologies and personal experiences that have propelled him to become one of the most recognized and respected vocal jazz specialists.

In this book, he brings into focus all of the detailed information necessary for the development of a vocal jazz ensemble. The subject of Zegree's passion, vocal jazz, is a genre that evolved out of "Jazz music (that) was born and raised in the United States." His book contains a treasury of practical and useful ideas Steve has accumulated during years of success. Any choral director would be remiss not to examine this book carefully as it is written by one of the best.

Dr. Eph Ehly
Kansas City, Missouri
August 2001

I was minding my own business, trying to relax in my hotel room in beautiful downtown Kalamazoo, when I got a phone call from Steve Zegree (he was no doctor back then). The Manhattan Transfer was performing the next evening and I was busily involved in something I like to call "a day off." Steve (grrrr...how did you get this number?!) immediately launched into his spiel about Gold Company and how the kids would love it if some of us would come hear a rehearsal and blah, blah, blah, they even do some Transfer tunes, and blah, blah, I could take you out to lunch..." Well, "lunch" being the operative word, I agreed to be picked up and taken to the college. He quite frankly wore me down with his relentless good cheer.

Let me say right from the top that I wish I had studied with Steve Zegree when I was in college. I was struck immediately by his passion for music, *all* music, his overwhelming enthusiasm, his communication with his students. My musical education was spotty, at best. I learned by doing, making mistakes, asking questions, teaching myself, reading books and certainly by listening. Guides appeared in my life at various junctures, but I found myself with holes in my musical skills which I am still trying to repair.

When I had the good fortune to meet Steve in Kalamazoo and see the amazing Gold Company program first-hand, I longed to enroll right then and there. First of all, Gold Company was the absolute best sounding, hippest college vocal jazz ensemble I had ever heard. And secondly, here was a comprehensive course of study that included everything a young professional singer would need: a solid basis in technique and theory (to eliminate all the "dumb singer" jokes), jazz history, microphone technique, how to perform, how to sing in the studio as opposed to live, vocal improvisation, how to develop your own phrasing and style, how to sing harmony, the skill of putting a set together, how to communicate with a band (the "dumb singer" thing again), how to use and understand audio and midi equipment without having a nervous breakdown — all the things I had to learn by trial and error.

Okay, I admit it; I also had a tinge of resentment. "These kids have it so easy; everything is laid out for them. Grumble, grumble...." I'm over it now and the good news is that all this information is available in this excellent teaching guide written by this most ardent, committed, and well-respected teacher of vocal music. As more music students and teachers, young and old alike, discover the richness of their own American musical heritage, they will need a book like this to lead them on their own journey of self- expression. And thanks, Steve for helping to keep vocal jazz alive.

Janis Siegel
New York City • August 2001

Preface

I am a classically trained musician. My formal music education was quite traditional — perhaps similar to yours. I started piano lessons at the age of seven, and it wasn't long before it was clear to everyone (especially me) that I had a very strong aversion to practicing. But somehow my parents were able to keep me on the piano bench long enough for me to make minimal progress. I seem to remember bribes and the dreaded egg timer set for fifteen minutes each day.

So, what kept my interest in music through my formative years when practicing was not much *fun* for me? The answer was: popular music (and eventually jazz). From an early age, I was encouraged by my father and my first piano teacher to play "by ear." This was a truly liberating and creative musical experience. It was *fun!* I wanted to *play* the piano much more than I wanted to *practice*. I now realize that there is nothing wrong with that attitude. As a matter of fact, what better activity for a child than "play"? I played and played on the piano, joined my first professional band in the seventh grade, and loved to try to figure out how to play the songs I heard on the radio.

My first exposure to jazz came through my older sister, who, as a high school student, listened to jazz (how extraordinary!). I was exposed to the jazz music of Ramsey Lewis, Les McCann, Dave Brubeck, and Herbie Hancock as much as any rock music that was popular with my friends. Although I had no formal education in jazz, I would sit at the piano and try to imitate the sounds I heard on those jazz recordings. Ironically, this was the traditional means of jazz education and the primary method of the dissemination of the jazz tradition. I had no idea what I was doing from a formal music and a theoretical perspective. However, as a result of my exposure to many, varied types of music, my musical growth and development consisted of classical training with an equal dose of improvisation.

So how, from this rather unremarkable start, did I come to write a book? There are actually two answers. The first is, "Someone asked me ." I do not think of myself as the book-writing type, but because enough people suggested that I undertake this project, I finally acquiesced. The second answer is that through teaching at the college level, I have developed a passion for music education. This is something that I find rather ironic in that none of my college degrees are in music education. As a matter of fact, I began my undergraduate studies as a political science major with the intention of becoming an attorney. Fortunately, (and just in time), I saw the light.

I ultimately majored in classical piano performance, mostly because over the years I had practiced (barely) enough piano to achieve some success on the instrument, and, because I could not sing. A dear friend and colleague used to describe me as having "a small, but ugly voice." With friends like that....

I have always enjoyed listening to the vocal instrument, and have spent a great deal of time accompanying classical singers and choral groups. As an accompanist I was able to hear the choir as a complete entity and able to gain insight into the thoughts and conducting styles of many gifted choral conductors. I have also accompanied solo singers and learned about the vocal instrument by sitting at the piano during lessons offered by some terrific voice teachers.

So where does vocal jazz enter my life? The answer is directly and indirectly connected to "the man who taught America to sing": Fred Waring. While a graduate student at Indiana University, I was invited to accompany the Fred Waring Music Workshops in Pennsylvania. There, I absorbed many of the styles and philosophies of Mr. Waring. After all, Mr. Waring had established a long and distinguished legacy of choral music excellence *and* commercial success (perhaps not the ultimate oxymoron!). He was a master showman who knew how to tailor his performances to the musical tastes of the general public without sacrificing quality or lowering his standards. His concerts would include enough diversity in programming for everyone to find *something* that they liked. Perhaps the greatest gift I received from Mr. Waring was the concept of a fast-paced program with universal appeal.

The second event that forever changed me regarding vocal jazz happened quite by accident. One summer while serving as pianist for the Waring Workshops I was in a musical phase where I was quite taken with the playing of jazz pianist Oscar Peterson. I wanted to listen to every recording of his that I could get my hands on. I was in a record store in Delaware Water Gap, **PA** and found a new album that featured Oscar Peterson with The Singers Unlimited. Although I had never heard of The Singers Unlimited, I nevertheless had to buy the album, because Oscar played on it! If you happen to know this recording you can imagine my initial reaction to hearing this music. If you love vocal and choral music and have never heard The Singers Unlimited, you owe it to yourself to immediately skip to the discography in this book (page 91), purchase a recording, and observe *your* reaction.

Upon completing my masters degree I was faced with that familiar question, "*now what*"? I knew that a career as a classical pianist was not for me, and I knew that I was not qualified to teach music at the secondary school level because I did not major in music education and was not certified. I also knew that I could find employment with America's royal families (Burger King and Dairy Queen), so I was not really too worried — I had something to fall back on! In fact, there was also another option. I had the opportunity to join a rock and roll band and tour as the group's pianist. That prospect had some appeal to me (as I had amassed much experience playing in bands), but a friend then suggested that I apply for a faculty position he had seen advertised by a university in Michigan. Until that time I had not even *considered* a career as a teacher, let alone at the university level. But I was urged by one of my professor-mentors to submit a resume and at the age of twenty-four was invited to audition for a position as a professor of music at Western Michigan University. To my surprise I was offered the job! Having rock-and-roll and Burger King as the other options, I chose the teaching gig, thinking to myself at the time that I would probably just commit to a nine month "trial period."

My first teaching assignment included private classical and jazz piano lessons, music theory, class piano, a jazz/pop music appreciation class and directing the "pop" vocal group. I thought it was a good sign that a large, diverse and high quality school of music would also include this kind of vocal group as a part of its curriculum. I also knew that I wanted to alter the focus of the group to concentrate on vocal jazz. At that time there were very few vocal jazz ensembles at the university level *anywhere*. There was a "hotbed" of vocal jazz at the secondary school and community college level in the Pacific Northwest and a few other programs throughout the country (Phil Mattson and Kirby Shaw were teaching at community colleges in California). However, there was certainly not much vocal jazz in the schools in the Midwest. I was geographically located in the heart of show choir territory. None of this deterred me however. My Fred Waring experience was still very fresh, and I was not opposed to choreography, but I knew that dancing would *not* be the focus of my ensemble for two reasons. First of all, my job was to teach music, and second, I was a terrible dancer! Over the years, I developed a philosophy for the Gold Company program at Western Michigan University that has allowed the ensemble to offer a variety of options for many different types of students. As a musician, as a music educator, as a choir director and as a vocal jazz director I set out to implement the following elements in the Gold Company program:

1 • Elevate the musicianship and musical skills of the ensemble members through the study of music theory and the development of keyboard competencies in conjunction with the study of vocal and choral techniques.

2 • Present our music in an exciting and energetic format. This includes some choreography as well as vocal jazz literature that is, at times, audience directed. Even though choreography is not emphasized, all the ensemble members participate. (This has proven to be very helpful for students who have gone on to work on Broadway or in other professional shows.)

3 • Sing with excellent jazz style while maintaining high traditional choral standards of tone quality, balance, blend and intonation.

4 • Utilize state of the art technology to help ensure that students keep up with the changing times.

5 • Emphasize professionalism and maturity in *all* aspects of their lives, musical and otherwise.

6 • Give students an opportunity to explore new areas of potential interest including arranging, composition, recording, solo singing, scat singing and improvisation, choreography (the choreography in Gold Company has traditionally been taught by students within the ensemble), business management and marketing, and sound systems.

The excitement, challenges, and growth that I have experienced as a result of directing a vocal jazz ensemble has not waned one iota over the years. I have had the good fortune of becoming friends with many members of my favorite professional vocal jazz groups including The Manhattan Transfer, Take 6, The Real Group, New York Voices, the Hi-Los and the Singers Unlimited. I am still convinced of the validity of the art form and all the good that can come as a result of pursuing this genre of music. It is hard work. It takes a tremendous effort on the part of all members of the ensemble. Sometimes I question whether all of the commitment of time, effort and energy is worth it. However, even as I write this, I eagerly look forward to the next rehearsal and the next musical challenge. I invite you to consider the concepts contained in this book and to apply them to your particular situation. Best of luck, don't give up, and enjoy the challenge!

Introduction

I recently completed running my first marathon. For those of you who might not be familiar with the physical and mental demands of this accomplishment, it took months of conditioning and a huge investment of time and energy to run this 26.2 mile event. What, you might ask, does my running a marathon have to do with a book on the subject of vocal jazz? Perhaps nothing, and perhaps everything.

Running a marathon is something I have always wanted to do, but there were many convenient reasons or excuses that (I thought) prevented me:

"I don't have the time to train."

"I can't make this a priority."

Or perhaps even, "I don't want to fail."

But now, at the ripe old age of, shall we say, "forty something," the time had come for me to put up or shut up. In other words, I had to take the plunge and go for it! The good news is that I lived to tell this story. The better news is that you can feel the same amount of personal growth and satisfaction I did by taking on a new, exciting and challenging endeavor. The process of learning to teach vocal jazz might take as long as it did for me to train for a marathon, but at least it won't be so hard on your feet and legs! The secret is to set your goal, take one step at a time (literally) and do not give up!

I have found that there are many people with the desire to know more about vocal jazz. Tremendous musical and personal satisfaction can be attained through the pursuit of vocal jazz excellence. You and your students can master harmonic and rhythmic complexities, improve aural and performance skills and have tons of fun (and perhaps an ounce of frustration) in the process. However, since the opportunities for any formal training in vocal jazz are presently rather limited, there are many highly qualified, skilled and talented choral directors who are interested and intrigued by the musical possibilities vocal jazz has to offer, but have no idea where to begin.

Well, now's the time for you to take the plunge and go for it! Please realize that in reading this book, you will be unmercifully subjected to my own opinions. Also though, realize that these opinions are based upon my own research and experiences, and that I do have a reason and justification for all the opinions and pedagogical suggestions that follow. It is possible (and encouraged for that matter) to disagree with any of these writings. The good news is that there are no absolutes in music, and we all need to be reminded to keep an open mind. Remember that it is the *process* that is most important. Let's have some fun together in the process!

CHAPTER ONE
What Is Vocal Jazz?

Teachers who wish to pursue the art of vocal jazz most likely fall into one of two categories. The first is the traditionally trained choral director who has extensive expertise in conducting and rehearsing concert choirs, classical solo voice training in the bel canto style of singing, a background in traditional music theory, and little or no exposure to the jazz idiom, jazz styles, and improvisation. The second is an instrumental musician with a jazz background who is probably inexperienced in the areas of traditional vocal and choral technique. Wherever you are in the spectrum between these two categories, it is important to note that anyone who has an interest in self-improvement, growth and development can overcome their deficiencies with focus and some hard work.

Remember: It's okay to admit to *not* knowing something! I hereby give you permission to plead ignorance on any subject, especially if you believe you *should* have knowledge about the subject. For example, I have earned three college degrees in music. Some people think that my keyboard skills are relatively well developed, and that I am a competent vocal jazz ensemble director. And yet, if someone asked me to create a beautiful sound on a violin, I would be utterly incapable. Even though I am a well-educated, gainfully employed professional musician, I cannot play the violin. Moreover, it would be silly of me to think that I could or should be able to play the violin, never having done so previously. If mastering the violin became a priority for me, I would have to first learn how to hold the instrument, and then I would need to establish a regimen of daily practice in order to develop the proper technique. At this point I would also have to be patient, because I would not initially be very accomplished, and the sounds emanating from my instrument would probably not be very satisfying. But after a period of several months (or years!), I would gradually learn the intricacies of the new instrument, and as a result find a new means of musical expression.

It's okay to admit to not knowing something!

I hope this analogy is not lost on the concert choir director with no previous vocal jazz experience. Initially, you will probably not be very skilled at the idiom, and that is okay! As long as you are willing to admit your inexperience, half the battle is already won.

As teachers, we are placed in the position of being "the source" of all information for our students. As a result, some of us have difficulty admitting to our students that we do not know the answer to a question, or that we have no experience in the area of expertise in question. Please consider "confessing" to your students that you don't have all the answers. Encouraging their involvement in the challenge of learning vocal jazz will allow them to feel a real sense of accomplishment as you reach your goals together.

Encouraging involvement in the challenge of learning vocal jazz will allow your students to feel a real sense of accomplishment as you reach your goals together.

Jazz instrumentalists also need to appreciate their skills and abilities, and then proceed on a course to shore up deficiencies. Usually these are in the areas of vocal/choral tone, proper vocal technique and knowledge of the vocal mechanism. One does not necessarily need to be an accomplished singer to be a successful choral conductor (I am living proof of that!), but knowledge of the voice and its mechanics is essential. Although voice lessons are not required, I strongly recommend them to anyone who would like to direct a choir and who has not studied privately.

DEFINING VOCAL JAZZ

Defining vocal jazz is a challenging prospect. There are many and varied opinions as to what constitutes a vocal jazz group. But in most cases, the vocal jazz ensemble is truly a choral ensemble grounded in the classical concert choir tradition. From a traditional choral perspective, the ensemble should sing fundamentally well, emphasizing healthy vocal technique, blend, balance, diction, intonation, and tone. The jazz aspect comes from the selection of repertoire (jazz compositions or arrangements in the jazz style), improvisation, and application of the appropriate style.

However, we must consider that some elements of jazz style (with West African derivations) and some elements of the Western European classical choral tradition are quite different. Therefore, opinions vary as to which stylistic elements are most important to a vocal jazz ensemble. Many believe the vocal jazz ensemble is simply a vocal extension of the instrumental big band. There are others who believe that vocal jazz is not possible without vocal improvisation. Still others believe vocal jazz can best be represented by a "jazzy sounding" a cappella arrangement that is sung with all of the musical elements that we associate with the traditional concert choir. As they say in Sweden, "vive la difference"! The musical expression will differ significantly in vocal ensembles that reflect these varied opinions, so how can we compare them? It's like comparing the recordings of Lambert, Hendricks and Ross to those of The Singers Unlimited. Lambert, Hendricks, and Ross were a trio of singers who sang swinging vocalese, improvised and used an instrumental jazz approach to their singing. The Singers Unlimited were a quartet who applied the recording studio technique of over-dubbing to choral arrangements which were beautifully sung using the traditional choral tenants of blend, balance and intonation. Indeed, the sonic differences between these ensembles are obvious, yet both are wonderful groups and both are important to vocal jazz. On a personal note, I absolutely love them both! Once again, it is crucial to get past our (possibly) somewhat limited perspectives and find the value, quality and artistry in every style of music. Again, I urge you to keep an open mind!

It is crucial to get past our limited perspectives and find the value, quality and artistry in every style of music.

It is important to note that the following section deals primarily in semantics. From my perspective, it does not matter what you call your ensemble, but how well they sing! There are several terms used to describe the types of vocal ensembles that specialize in jazz or "popular" music. They include:

VOCAL JAZZ ENSEMBLE

The term "vocal jazz" is used to describe the genre that generally refers to small choral ensembles that specialize in jazz. These ensembles range from a *vocal combo* of four to nine singers to a *vocal jazz ensemble* of 10 to 24 singers all the way up to a *jazz choir* with 26 to 100 or more voices. Because extra-musical considerations (choreography, etc) are usually not an important part of the presentation, the advanced vocal jazz ensemble can pursue repertoire that presents quite a challenge to the singers' aural and rhythmic skills. Vocal jazz literature is available for all levels of ability, from children's choir to professional groups and an increasing number of colleges and universities are developing degree programs in jazz studies that include vocal jazz.

SHOW CHOIR

The *show choir* typically combines choral music with elaborate choreography and staging. The idiom is more representative of the musical theatre genre and performances can often resemble large production numbers from a Broadway musical, complete with costume changes and elaborate sets. When a group chooses to emphasize choreography over singing, the overall complexity of the choral music is usually decreased, and sometimes the group's blend, balance and intonation can be adversely affected by the physical demands of the dancing. For programming contrast, many show choirs include a ballad or even some vocal jazz repertoire in their program. Usually these pieces are staged, but not choreographed and as a result can highlight the vocal artistry of the ensemble.

Show choirs are most frequently found at the middle school and high school levels. As a result, most choral students will have their peak show choir experience at this level. Most colleges and universities are unwilling to commit the resources required to administer a show choir program, and a show choir has no degree significance in most college music programs. Additionally, serious music students are not willing (nor should they be!) to spend vast amounts of time practicing choreography when they need to be practicing piano, voice, and improving their musical skills. One notable exception is the musical theatre major that indeed needs to develop singing, dancing and acting skills in preparation for a performance career. Many universities offer a degree program in musical theatre, or at least offer opportunities through musical productions so that students can develop and improve their acting, singing and dancing competencies.

SWING CHOIR

Swing choir is a term that describes a vocal group that emphasizes pop literature and probably adds a small amount of motion or choreography to the performance. This term is probably a bit outdated (similar to the term *stage band* to describe the contemporary instrumental jazz ensemble). The swing choir generally performs music that is similar to the repertoire of vocal jazz ensembles and show choirs.

Although there are obvious and distinct differences in vocal jazz ensembles and show choirs, in the interest of time and efficiency, from this point on I will use the term "vocal jazz ensemble" as an all-inclusive term, which includes show choirs, swing choirs and vocal jazz groups of all sizes.

JUSTIFICATION: WHY VOCAL JAZZ?

Vocal jazz is probably the newest and most dynamic trend in choral music education. Traditional concert choir literature has been sung for over 500 years. Jazz choir literature has been applied in academic settings for only some thirty years, and most choral musicians are still relatively inexperienced in the vocal jazz style. The current evolution of vocal jazz programs in schools is similar to the development of instrumental jazz programs during the late 1970's.

Vocal jazz is probably the newest and most dynamic trend in choral music education.

Due in large part to the popularity of touring and recording big bands led by Buddy Rich, Maynard Ferguson, Stan Kenton and Woody Herman during the 1970's and early 80's, many high school and college students were very interested in playing this style of music. Almost overnight, band directors with little or no jazz experience found themselves responsible for a stage band or jazz ensemble. Over the years, with the help of jazz education advocates such as Jamey Aebersold, David Baker and Jerry Coker, excellent performance standards and repertoire were developed for instrumental jazz groups of all ability levels. Today, most high schools and colleges include instrumental jazz as an integral part of their overall music program. A similar situation is emerging in vocal jazz education, with more and more teachers and administrators acknowledging the importance of including this music as a part of a total choral program, and several publishing companies working to expand the amount of quality literature available. The concept that "jazz is a four-letter word" is one that, thankfully, is rapidly becoming outmoded in music education.

The concept that "jazz is a four-letter word" is one that, thankfully, is rapidly becoming outmoded in music education.

Music education programs everywhere are being threatened, cut back or even eliminated. Therefore, it is imperative that we can successfully defend and justify our choices for curriculum and programming. Your decision to teach vocal jazz can be justified on several levels:

1 • Jazz music was born and raised in the United States. It is our unique musical contribution to the world. Although it is important to study classical music history and theory from a Western European tradition, as well as music from other regions and cultures throughout the world, jazz is the one musical idiom that is viewed as American in origin. Jazz is art music (as opposed to pop or commercial music) and is taken very seriously by the people who practice and perform it.

2 • The source of much of our jazz repertoire is the songs written by the great American songwriters. Composers such as George Gershwin, Duke Ellington, Richard Rodgers, Irving Berlin, Cole Porter, Jerome Kern, and Harold Arlen (and their lyricists) are responsible for the art songs of our country and of the 20th century. Artistically, we can equate these songs with Italian art songs and the 19th century lieder of Schubert, Schumann, Liszt, Brahms and Wolf. Like their classical predecessors, the great American standard songs have beautiful melodies and great harmonies that are set to wonderful texts (in English!). It is imperative that we celebrate and perpetuate the artistry of the great American composers and lyricists.

3 • The stylistic elements found in vocal jazz can be quite challenging to your singers. The rhythms, harmonic complexities, and opportunities for improvisation will undoubtedly develop your singers' aural skills and improve their overall musicianship.

4 • It is quite likely that the vocal jazz ensemble will become a popular and "hip" part of your total choral program. However, it is important to emphasize that the concert choir should be the cornerstone and foundation of your choral program. Fundamentals, philosophies, concepts, and all things musical must first be taught in the concert choir setting. The vocal jazz ensemble should be a vital and important part of your choral program, but not at the expense of the concert choir. I urge you to consider selecting only the best singer/musicians, the most mature leaders, and the nicest people from your concert choir to form the vocal jazz ensemble. As a result, participation in the vocal jazz group will carry an air of prestige, and younger singers will strive to develop and improve their musical skills and abilities with

the hope of some day singing in the vocal jazz ensemble.

The vocal jazz ensemble can serve many purposes beyond the valuable music education your students will experience. It can serve the community as an ambassador of the school and can help recruit and attract more students to your choral program. After all, we all know that students are continually striving to raise their **HQ**,[1] and what better way than through the pursuit of musical excellence through vocal jazz?!

---

[1]Your **HQ** is the cool counterpart to your **IQ** (Intelligence Quotient). For us, **HQ** stands for *Hipness Quotient!*

*The short cut to
success is hard work.
Starting today.*

CHAPTER 2

Roots and Traditions

The history of vocal groups in America can be traced as far back as the Revolutionary War. American composer William Billings organized singing schools that taught the basics of ensemble singing. Vocal groups consisted of harmony singers: vocalists who created an ensemble sound rather than functioning as soloists. During the 19th century, popular vocal groups emerged from travelling minstrel shows. Spiritual groups such as the Fisk Jubilee Singers gained international recognition. Barbershop quartets were also quite popular at the end of the 19th century and as vaudeville developed, vocal groups became a prominent part of the show. Even though the recording industry was in its infancy, vocal groups in the 1890's reached a wide audience thanks to early recordings (little could Thomas Edison anticipate the technological future of his invention!).

In the 1920's the surging popularity of radio broadcasts brought about changes in the general public's perception of popular music. Big bands, jazz ensembles and vocal soloists became more popular, and the harmonies of vocal groups became more sophisticated. In the 1930's, the Boswell Sisters, the Rhythm Boys and the Mills Brothers were influential in the development of this new genre. The great instrumental arrangements and orchestrations of Louis Armstrong and Duke Ellington inspired the Mills Brothers whose combination of vocal imitations of instruments with sophisticated harmonies served as the inspiration for many of the vocal groups who followed, most notably the Ink Spots.

At the same time, the church was another source of close vocal harmony. The development of gospel music from the spiritual tradition brought about notable groups such as the Golden Gate Jubilee Quartet and the Dixie Hummingbirds. These ensembles, although usually based in the church, also sang secular music that reached a much wider audience. The style of music in the sacred and secular idioms was so similar that frequently the text was the only distinguishing factor. This tradition continues today, as many times the only characteristic distinguishing contemporary Christian and gospel literature from pop, rhythm and blues and vocal jazz is the subject matter.

The Big Band era reached its heyday in the 1940's, when dance bands commonly included a vocal group. The Andrews Sisters, the Modernaires, the Pied Pipers and the Delta Rhythm Boys were some of the more popular vocal ensembles of that era. The great jazz vocalist Mel Torme collaborated with his group the Mel-Tones in the 1940's to create a forward-looking vocal jazz group. The sophisticated harmonic language and complex arrangements Torme brought to his ensemble created a new vocabulary that included jazz elements, and as a result, jazz began to be successfully incorporated into the domain of traditional choral groups. It was a time when good music was popular and popular music was good!

*It was a time
when good music was
popular and popular
music was good!*

In the early 1950's, solo singers King Pleasure and Eddie Jefferson were credited with popularizing "vocalese." This art form involves writing original lyrics and applying them to previously recorded instrumental jazz solos. Using these lyrics, the singer would recreate the original instrumental solo, matching all the pitches, inflections and style. Jazz fans and critics alike refer to Lambert, Hendricks and Ross as one the greatest vocal jazz groups ever because they did so much to perfect the art of vocalese and were able to reach a worldwide audience. Another ensemble, Le Double Six de Paris developed a similar style in France. One of the members of Le Double Six was Ward Swingle who formed The Swingle Singers in the early 1960's. The Swingles initially achieved worldwide popularity by singing vocal jazz arrangements of the instrumental music of J.S. Bach. Since those early Bach recordings, the group has expanded its repertoire to include choral music from all eras, including avant garde and (of course) vocal jazz.

Also in the 1950's, the Four Freshmen emerged with a new sound that influenced other male vocal groups, including the Hi-Lo's (and even the Beach Boys!). These groups exhibited a newer, fresher harmonic vocabulary that included more open voicings, chord extensions and the substitution of other chord tones for the root.

The Singers Unlimited, representing a logical progression from the Hi-Lo's, began making records in the 1970's. Both groups included Gene Puerling as a singer and as the principal vocal arranger. The Singers Unlimited consisted of four Chicago-based studio (jingle) singers who used the recording studio process of over-dubbing to create a larger choral sound and to sing thicker than four-part textures.

The Manhattan Transfer is another important vocal jazz ensemble, especially to vocal ensembles in school music programs. The Transfer began their remarkably successful tenure as a vocal group in the 1970's. This quartet has probably had the greatest impact on the dissemination of vocal jazz literature to the choral music education world through their recorded and published arrangements (including *Operator, Birdland, Ray's Rockhouse, How High The Moon, Java Jive and Trickle, Trickle*), which have become standards in the vocal jazz repertoire. Recently, harmony groups such as Take 6, New York Voices, and Sweden's The Real Group have served to create musical excellence in vocal jazz while also establishing a profound influence on the music education scene.

It is also noteworthy to mention vocal groups such as the King's Singers and Chanticleer. While these a cappella groups are known primarily as classical vocal ensembles specializing in music from the Renaissance era, each has made recordings of vocal jazz arrangements. Audiences often anxiously await the concluding portion of these groups' live performances, as they invariably include selections from their vocal jazz repertoire.

Fortunately, we now have easy access to recordings made by most of these groups (see Appendix I: Vocal Jazz Discography on page 91). Even though recording technology was in its infancy at the time the Mills Brothers and Boswell Sisters made most of their recordings, they still warrant a good listen. When listening to recordings made by the Hi-Lo's in the 1950's, I am amazed at the musical accuracy and artistic beauty of the singing, especially when realizing that these recordings were made live! While recording studio technology and computers help to produce some incredible recordings today, these vintage and historically important recordings continue to be an excellent source of education and inspiration to fans, teachers and students of vocal jazz.

CHAPTER 3

Vocal Jazz: It's a Matter of Style!

I am a very fortunate person! I have had the opportunity to travel throughout the world sharing music either as conductor, pianist or clinician. Universally, I encounter people who say to me, "Steve, I would love to do vocal jazz, but...

I don't think my students would like it.

It's just too hard.

I'm rhythmically-challenged.

I don't understand what all those squiggly lines in the music mean.

I can't scat sing.

I really need to do my laundry."

One of my philosophies of music education is making musical information as easy to understand as possible for my students. After all, I teach at the university level! To do this, I try to break down all the elements to the lowest common denominator (**LCD**). By focusing on one element at a time, it is easier to dispel the mystery of how to make the music happen, and the process becomes less threatening and more accessible to more people. As a result, more students (and educators) are willing and able to stretch their wings, attempt new things and enjoy what the new music brings! The good news is that you *can* teach vocal jazz, and in fact, it is not that difficult. Vocal jazz is simply a style of music within the entire spectrum and long history of choral literature. Just as one might plan to approach the stylistic interpretation of a Renaissance motet or madrigal differently than a motet by Brahms or Bruckner, there are stylistic elements that are indigenous to vocal jazz. At the lowest common denominator, there are basically three styles of music within vocal jazz: swing, latin and ballad. Once you understand the concepts and elements that characterize each style, you will be ready to accept the challenge of teaching the music. The stylistic elements that characterize vocal jazz include:

There are basically three styles of music within vocal jazz: swing, latin and ballad.

SWING

Swing is one of the stylistic characteristics that is essential to the interpretation of jazz. Although difficult to define, it is a term that applies to the rhythmic aspects of the music. You can listen to a vocal jazz ensemble that sings very well, yet swings very poorly! And keep in mind, swing has nothing to do with the forces (vocal or instrumental) that are performing. A group can swing when singing a cappella, or not swing when singing with instrumental accompaniment. In order for the music to swing there should be:

Syncopation. The jazz style is characterized by a strong sense of syncopation. Syncopation can perhaps best be described as the accenting of notes that take place either just before or just after the beat. In a macro sense, this means accenting beats two and four when (as in classical music) the listener is anticipating accents on beats one and three. One of the most important initial factors in instilling a sense of swing in the vocal ensemble is to develop their ability to comfortably and confidently snap their fingers on beats two and four. This seemingly simple task can in fact be quite challenging. A vast majority of the classical music we have studied and learned emphasizes beats one and three. Most jazz music (as well as pop, rock, funk and gospel) emphasizes the backbeat, or a stronger pulse on beats two and four. A good practice aid to help instill confidence for this feel is the jazz metronome — it only clicks on two and four…(okay, I'm kidding). But, I do believe there is a natural, physical response which feels good when snapping fingers or tapping toes on beats two and four to a medium swing jazz groove. It is something that cannot be assimilated only by reading a book; you must experience it. So, put on the **CD** right now and try it!

♪ EXAMPLE 3.1

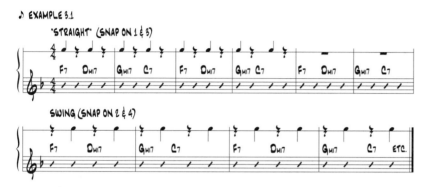

Swinging eighth notes. In many vocal jazz scores (commonly referred to as *charts* by jazz musicians) the tempo indication is often followed by:

EXAMPLE 3.2

It is important to realize that both the eighth and dotted eighth-sixteenth notations are interpreted the same way; the accent is on the off-beat eighth note, and that is the shortest part of the beat. To most classically trained musicians, this may initially feel very uncomfortable; however, there are several selections of music from the classical repertoire that serve as an example of the swing feel. One is Ferde Grofe's *On the Trail* from "Grand Canyon Suite." This rhythmic feel can also be described as a $\frac{12}{8}$ time signature with beats one and two, four and five, seven and eight, and ten and eleven tied, and a slight accent on three, six, nine, and twelve:

EXAMPLE 3.3

Of course jazz is an aural language, so the best way for you and your students to assimilate the swing style is to listen to jazz as much as possible (see Appendix I: Vocal Jazz Discography on page 91 for ideas and suggestions). With a bit of practice and repetition most people will develop an understanding as well as a natural feel for this concept.

The interpretation of swing in the vocal jazz ensemble is essentially the same as it is in instrumental music. I suggest that you spend some time with an experienced jazz ensemble director and perhaps even invite them to a rehearsal to offer suggestions to your choir on the interpretation of jazz notation. (Note: Dare I suggest that you consider the band director in your own school?)

Of course jazz is an aural language, so the best way for you and your students to assimilate the swing style is to listen to jazz as much as possible.

A *constant, consistent tempo.* You must establish the tempo in your mind prior to the start of the piece. A metronome can be a great aid if there are any doubts about finding "the perfect tempo," especially in a performance situation where nerves or other distractions can serve to detract from usually clear thinking. Do your best to teach all singers and players to develop an internal clock to feel the same tempo. I frequently rehearse a vocal jazz ensemble a cappella, even on pieces with instrumental accompaniment. This reinforces the importance of the singers developing confidence in their rhythmic feel, as well as rhythmic independence, so that relying on instrumental accompaniment for a constant tempo becomes unnecessary. This technique makes it much easier to combine the singers with the instrumentalists, ensuring an even stronger sense of constant tempo. I also encourage my students to practice independently with a metronome, so that the steady beat is constantly reinforced. The ultimate goal is for a piece of music to end in approximately the same tempo it began! The excerpt from *One in a Million* is an excellent illustration of how a straight ahead swing chart should sound. Pay special attention to the rhythmic placement of the eighth notes.

♪ EXAMPLE 3.3A (FROM "ONE IN A MILLION", TRACK 2)

LATIN STYLE

Latin is a general term used to describe music with stylistic elements from countries in South America, Central America, and the Caribbean.

Latin is a general term used to describe music with stylistic elements from countries in South America, Central America, and the Caribbean. The **LCD** to interpreting music in this style is to sing and play even eighth notes (as opposed to "swinging" eighth notes). In this context latin refers to the Latin American region, not the traditional language of the Roman Catholic Church.

Just as the word "car" can be used to describe many different types and models of automobiles, Latin is a generic term used to describe many vastly different styles of music. Other more specific words used to describe this style of music include *Bossa Nova, Samba, Afro-Cuban, Afro-Caribbean,* and *Salsa.* Studying and listening to the indigenous music of the Cuban salsa, Brazilian bossa nova and samba, Argentinean tango, Jamaican reggae, Trinidadian calypso and the musics of other South and Central-American countries will reveal a wide variety of stylistic differences. The following dances, rhythms and terms warrant a closer examination in order to raise your Latin **HQ**:

Bossa Nova. This is one of the most popular beats found in contemporary jazz. It is primarily of Brazilian descent and generally interpreted as a medium tempo, straight eighth note feel using a rhythmic pattern as follows:

♪ EXAMPLE 3.4

Samba. Another very popular dance form from Brazil, the samba is generally a faster tempo than the bossa nova with a double-time feel and the sixteenth note (or eighth note in cut time) providing the underlying pulse.

♪ EXAMPLE 3.5

One of the most common rhythmic patterns that can serve as the underlying foundation of a bossa nova or samba piece is the partito alto, indicated below.

♪ EXAMPLE 3.6

Combining the samba groove with the partito alto gives this style of music its unique flavor.

Salsa. This style of latin jazz has roots in Cuba and Puerto Rico. This dance form is composed of several elements, each with a specific name and specific function.

Son clave or just *clave* (pronounced *clah*-vay) is a specific two-bar rhythmic pattern that is the underlying foundation for this music. This pattern occurs in two forms: three and two, or two and three.

The clave is also a musical instrument. It is a pair of short, thick sticks, which when hit together, create the distinctive clave sound. Every other component of the salsa style must be in sync with the clave pattern. This pattern also appears as the underlying rhythmic foundation for other styles of music including Dixieland, rhythm and blues, funk, fusion, pop and even musical theatre (think about the groove on "Hand Jive" from the musical *Grease)*.

EXAMPLE 3.7

Montuno is a repeated two, four or eight bar rhythmic and melodic/harmonic vamp; pattern or ostinato typically played on the piano.

EXAMPLE 3.8

Tumbao is the pattern played by the bass player. Most tumbaos accent the fourth beat of each bar, and *do not* play on beat one!

EXAMPLE 3.9

This concept of playing and time feel differs significantly from the jazz swing style, and most likely will have to be practiced by the bass player before it can be mastered.

There are several additional percussion instruments that typically can be played in salsa music, including timbales, conga drums, bongo drums, guiro and cowbell. Each of these instruments plays a different specific rhythm, all relating to the underlying clave rhythm.

Remember that most Latin music, while frequently rhythmically complex, is repetitious. As in most dance music, one of the main factors for a successful performance is to just let it groove! Make sure that your students resist the urge to overplay or over sing. In latin music, less *is* more! Simply learn the appropriate rhythms and patterns and do not vary them. In this case the **LCD** will also guarantee the most stylistic authenticity. Example 3.10 (track six on the **CD**) is an excerpt from *This Masquerade* that demonstrates this concept.

♪ EXAMPLE 3.10 THIS MASQUERADE (MEASURE 5)

BALLAD

The third basic style in vocal jazz is the ballad. Ballads can be performed a cappella with rubato or in tempo. They may be accompanied, and might feature a vocal and/or instrumental soloist. I am a strong advocate of all vocal jazz ensembles programming an a cappella ballad in their repertoire. The ballad is the best way for a traditionally trained concert choir director to gain experience in the vocal jazz idiom, as there are essentially no differences between the interpretation of an a cappella ballad and a selection of a cappella literature from the traditional choral repertoire. Both styles require a strict reading of the written harmonies and rhythms, employing the traditional concepts of blend, balance, intonation, tonal production, vowel unification, and diction. The a cappella ballad provides the ultimate challenge for the choral musician. Take away the instrumental accompaniment, take away the choreography, and you are left with a choral ensemble. This is the time to determine just how well (from the traditional choral perspective) a vocal jazz ensemble can sing. Also, the a cappella ballad presents a terrific opportunity and challenge for the conductor to utilize conducting technique, and for both conductor and singers to achieve artistic integrity and interpretive creativity.

I am a strong advocate of all vocal jazz ensembles programming an a cappella ballad in their repertoire.

In general, one of the most important factors in determining the quality of a piece of choral music is the text. When selecting a ballad, select a text that is age appropriate for the maturity level of your ensemble. If the ensemble can understand and relate to the subject matter, the rehearsal process and ultimate performance will be greatly enhanced. Let the musical line and a thoughtful, speech-like delivery of the lyric be your inspiration for interpretation, especially in ballads. Also, *take your time!* Many directors are uncomfortable with an interpretation that includes a slower tempo and rubato, but this is one of the most important elements that will add musicianship and maturity to the performance. Please note that every aspect of ballad interpretation suggested above applies equally to vocal jazz ensembles and traditional concert choirs.

It is important to remember that all printed music is just that: printed music. Ink on paper. The music takes place first in your mind, then it is your obligation to effectively communicate your thoughts to those who will be performing the music. The ink on paper needs to be interpreted, and in the popular ballad you have the greatest amount of freedom to alter rhythms, lengthen phrases, and employ rubato to create motion and, as a result, musically and emotionally express the text. The excerpt from *But Beautiful* (track seven on the **CD**) in example 3.11 demonstrates some of these ideas.

♪ EXAMPLE 3.11 (FROM BUT BEAUTIFUL, MEAS 25)

Love is tear - ful,____ so they say. It's a prob - lem____ or it's

play.____ It's a heart - ache____ ei - ther way,____ but beau - ti - ful.____

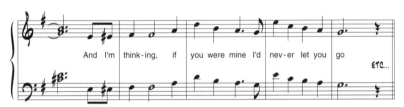

And I'm think - ing, if you were mine I'd nev - er let you go ETC...

Music by Jimmy Van Heusen Words by Johnny Burke
Copyright © 1947 (Renewed) by Onyx Music Corporation (ASCAP) and Bourne Co.
All rights to Onyx Music Corporation administered by Music Sales Corporation (ASCAP)
International Copyright Secured. All Rights Reserved.
Reprinted by permission.

Overall Stylistic Considerations for Vocal Jazz

MINIMAL VIBRATO

Just as one might consider the minimization of vibrato in singing certain types of music from the Renaissance era, one should consider minimizing the vibrato in the jazz style. Please note that nowhere in this book (other than in this sentence) will you see the term "straight tone." I prefer the concept of "minimized vibrato." And, contrary to the opinion held by some teachers of voice, choral singing that involves minimizing the vibrato does not in any way cause harm to the vocal mechanism.

The main reason to consider the minimization of vibrato is the fact that a great deal of vocal jazz literature involves very close harmony between the inner voices. In order to achieve sonic clarity with jazz harmony, vibrato must be minimized. Let's take a look at example 3.12 (track eight on the CD), and listen to it with vibrato, and then with minimized vibrato.

♪ EXAMPLE 3.12 (FROM THIS MASQUERADE, MEAS. 21)

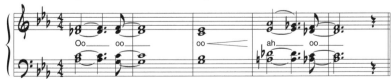

Oo____ oo____ oo____ ah____ oo____

I'm sure that you can hear the difference in harmonic clarity between the two examples. But, vibrato does not have to be eliminated entirely, and in fact could be used at the end of phrases, or as a part of the melody. It is also stylistically appropriate to use a fuller vibrato when singing in the gospel or pop idioms, or when featured as soloist within the vocal jazz ensemble. When listening to the vocal groups listed in the discography, focus your attention on the singers' use of vibrato. Note how much (if any) is used, and specifically when and where. You may be surprised to hear, at times, how much vibrato is used, especially in smaller professional groups. Remember that there is no right or wrong when it comes to use of vibrato. It is simply a matter of personal preference and taste, although, as mentioned above, close harmonies will probably necessitate the minimization of vibrato to achieve tonal clarity and precise intonation within the vocal jazz ensemble.

TONAL FLEXIBILITY

Whether conducting a concert choir or a vocal jazz ensemble, I am always interested in celebrating the tonal uniqueness of the human voice and the individual singer.

Achieving the "appropriate" sound in the vocal jazz style is an area that, again, engenders a wide variety of differing opinions. Whether conducting a concert choir or a vocal jazz ensemble, I am always interested in celebrating the tonal uniqueness of the human voice and the individual singer. Therefore, it would be possible (and likely) that the same group of singers would sound like a completely different ensemble from one piece of music to another. When a pianist plays a note on the piano, they can play that note with dynamic variety and with varied articulation, but the *tone* of that note is inflexible and will remain constant. The vocalist, on the other hand, can sing the same note with a huge palette of tonal variety. Some of these variants might include: head voice vs. chest voice or appropriate mix, amount of vibrato, vowel formation, maturity of sound, ratio of breath to tone, placement and degree of resonance. Just as we might choose to teach our concert choir to create differing approaches to the tone in choral literature from the 16th and 19th centuries, it would be equally appropriate (and desirable) to have the vocal jazz ensemble sound different when singing repertoire in the jazz or gospel style. A close listening of excellent representative vocal groups in each of these idioms will offer a sonic model that your students can also hear, and, when appropriate , emulate and imitate!

ARTICULATIONS AND SPECIAL EFFECTS

The "special effects" (markings in the score such as shakes, glissandos, smears, and breath accents) that contribute to creating a more stylistically correct vocal jazz sound should be one of the smallest concerns on the journey down the path to vocal jazz success.

EXAMPLE 3.13

LONG FALL   SHAKE (SMALL OR LARGE)   BREATH ACCENT

SCOOP   QUICK FALL   GLISS

These stylistic elements are fun to add and very easy to achieve. The excerpt from *Doctor Blues* in example 3.13A (track nine on the **CD**) demonstrates some of these effects.

♪ EXAMPLE 3.13 (CD TRACK #9) FROM DOCTOR BLUES, MEAS. 17

Think of these inflections like the cherry on top of a hot fudge sundae. It's not really necessary, but it does add a bit of color and flavor. If you love ice cream as much as I do, you know that what is *under* the cherry is what is really important — the whipped cream, nuts, hot fudge, ice cream, and the container for the entire sundae. All of those things are much more important than the cherry. As a matter of fact, some people don't even want the cherry with their sundae, and that is quite all right.

It is still a good sundae. In a vocal jazz chart, learning the correct notes, rhythms, harmonies and lyrics with accurate blend, balance, tone and intonation is much more important than the special effects. The effects can be added later in the rehearsal process.

Most of the effects in a vocal jazz chart are added to achieve a more authentic jazz style. They often originate from the stylistic elements of the instrumental jazz ensemble or the effects that solo jazz and pop singers use in their individual interpretations of songs. Because the human voice has so much flexibility, use of glissandos, scoops, and shakes are completely natural and accessible to the solo singer or the vocal group, regardless of age and experience.

DICTION

Like many aspects of choral music, diction is an area where there can be as many opinions as there are conductors. I believe that the approach to diction in the vocal jazz idiom should differ from that of the traditional concert choir. As you might expect, I have developed several reasons for this, and I hope that you will consider applying these concepts as you work with your own group. It is likely that the vocal jazz literature you teach will be in English, but there is also vocal jazz repertoire in French, Portugese, German, Latin, and Spanish.

When singing jazz and popular literature in English, the ensemble should use the vernacular and pronounce words as they would in their natural speech.

When singing jazz and popular literature in English, the ensemble should use the vernacular and pronounce words as they would in their natural speech. This is a concept that was favored by Fred Waring through his use of *tone-syllables*. There are still published vocal arrangements that include tone-syllables below the English text. Although the tone syllables appear to be a foreign language, the intended result is that the ensemble will sing in completely clear, intelligible, and unaffected English.

There are many concert choir directors who apply British English and/or Italian vowels to the English diction they teach to their choirs. In English vernacular, the word "it" does not sound like the word "eat." I believe the word "it" should rhyme with the word "hit." While many concepts of blend, balance and intonation can be assisted by good diction, these concepts will not be impeded when the choir sings natural, speech-like English. One of the biggest English diction challenges is the diphthong. In the jazz style as in the classical choral style it is best to unify the initial vowel sound, then resolve the diphthong as an ensemble, perhaps giving more time and emphasis to the consequent vowel sound.

Also, in the concert choir we tend to explode and exaggerate consonants. While this adds drama and clarity to concert choir diction, it is not as appropriate for the vocal jazz ensemble. When an ensemble is singing with microphones (especially close-mic singing), consonants must be de-emphasized. The plosive and sibilant consonants explode air that results in an unpleasant and uncharacteristic sound and the popping of "p's" and the hissing of "s's" also needs to be minimized — a technique that singers should learn and apply to their jazz and pop English diction.

A close examination of the diction used by most professional vocal jazz ensembles will reveal a strict adherence to the concepts suggested above. I always try to allow good taste and the desire that our audiences can clearly and easily understand the meaning of the text to be my underlying guide to English diction.

CONDUCTING GESTURES

The role of the conductor in the vocal jazz ensemble should vary significantly from that of the concert choir director. First, the jazz choir director must master the art of the *count off*. The count off is the best (and hippest) way to start a piece of music that has a constant tempo, whether in swing or latin style. When counting off a swing tune, determine the tempo of the piece (with or without the help of a metronome), establish finger snaps on beats two and four, then count off crisply as follows: "One, (snap), two, (snap), one, two, three, four…." There is no need to beat a traditional four pattern, as the singers, if well prepared, will take care of themselves and your conducting gestures will most likely get in the way. When directing Gold Company, I spend as much time in the geographical area of the rhythm section as I do in front of the vocal ensemble. My preference is to remove myself from the center of attention, thereby allowing a more immediate connection between the audience and the performers. Of course, there are times in swing and latin tunes when the conductor must be in front of the vocal ensemble. At these times, simply walk to center stage and use the appropriate gestures.

A cappella ballads present greater conducting opportunities and challenges for the vocal jazz director. The conducting styles and gestures for a cappella ballads in the vocal jazz ensemble can be essentially the same as in the concert choir setting. Many ensembles choose to perform their ballad without a conductor (I have heard many ensembles sing a cappella ballads beautifully without the benefit of a conductor), but it is usually my preference to conduct the ballad. Consider that with no conductor, the singers can easily function on mental and musical auto-pilot, allowing their intellectual, artistic and musical expression to become disengaged, especially after several performances of the same tune. I have found that the presence of the conductor allows for greater mental focus and potential artistic spontaneity in the interpretation and performance of an a cappella ballad.

External factors can also affect the need to slightly alter or change the interpretation of the ballad. For example, the acoustics of the performance venue should be considered. A room with substantial reverberation may dictate a slower interpretation and longer pauses at phrase endings. On a day when the ensemble is singing particularly well, the conductor can add spontaneity and subtle changes that can serve to transform a mundane moment into a magical one. At the same time, it is important for the conductor to realize that the music is the most important aspect of the performance, not the person conducting! Make sure you do not get in the way; just remember to think of yourself as the facilitator of the music making process.

It is also important to remember that your best conducting takes place in your rehearsal. Some of my most satisfying conducting experiences occur during a performance when, in the middle of a song, I can walk to the side of the stage and enjoy with great pride the performance of the ensemble.

Whether it is swing, latin, ballad, gospel, funk, pop, renaissance, baroque, romantic, or avant-garde, it is *all* simply a matter of style. The basic tenets of choral musicianship (blend, balance, intonation) can be applied to all styles of music, from classical to jazz. Within the classical choral world one can find a large variety of styles, a wide variety of opinions on interpretation, and many different approaches to choral tone. The same variety can be applied to vocal jazz. It is the responsibility of the conductor to be as fully informed from an historical, musical, technical, and stylistic perspective as possible. When the knowledge of appropriate style is combined with basic musicianship, fundamental musical skills and effective rehearsal technique, the final product will invariably result in wonderful music making.

The conducting styles and gestures for a cappella ballads in the vocal jazz ensemble can be essentially the same as in the concert choir setting.

Students will rise
to your level
of expectation.
Avoid sinking
to theirs...

CHAPTER 4

Rehearsal Techniques For The Vocal Jazz Ensemble: How Do They Differ From Traditional Concepts?

The rehearsal: a magical place! This is where the director meets the ensemble and faces the awesome responsibility of educating and enlightening the singers and as a direct result, generating improvement in the ensemble. This chapter includes an overview of the musical abilities that a vocal jazz director needs and some specific ways to prepare for and run a vocal jazz rehearsal (see Appendix II: Rehearsal Prep Guide on page 104).

The following exercise is one of my favorite ways to begin a rehearsal with a novice vocal jazz group. It opens their ears and helps to show them that singing jazz harmonies is truly an attainable goal.

FROM BACH TO TAKE 6 (TRACK 10 ON THE CD)

The stylistic elements found in the four part choral writing of J.S. Bach provide the basis for the common practice studied in most colleges and universities. Although this writing style (and the rules of part-writing and voice-leading associated with it) has gained universal acceptance in the world of traditional choral music, it has little bearing on most of the writing and arranging in the vocal jazz style. Example 4.1 shows a traditional voicing of a G major triad:

In jazz arranging we tend to favor four part texture, with no pitches doubled (refer to Chapter 5 for more information). To change the quality of the G major chord above to a dominant seventh chord, the most obvious way to create the new chord is to lower the soprano pitch by a whole step:

However, there is another, less obvious, solution to this problem. A vocal jazz arranger would probably lower the bass note to F and leave the soprano on G. That way there are 4 parts with no pitches doubled, and, a much cooler sounding chord:

We will learn in Chapter 6 (The Rhythm Section), the root of the chord is often played by the double bass, so the voicing in example 4.3 makes perfect sense. In an a cappella chart there might be a fifth part added as in example 4.3A.

Play 4.2 and 4.3 on the piano and listen to how dramatically different they sound, even though the "reorganization" of the notes is ever so slight. This alternate solution to creating a dominant seventh chord highlights two of the perceived difficulties in singing vocal jazz:

1 • The basses are singing the seventh of the chord — what's up with that? Everybody and their grandmother know that basses were born and raised to sing roots!

2 • The interval between the bass and tenor is the dreaded tritone. These two notes are the third and seventh of the chord so they are the most important notes in the chord because they determine the quality of the chord.

Once you are able to recognize this voicing of the dominant seventh chord and your men are comfortable singing it, many vocal jazz arrangements will be much more accessible for your ensemble.

This brings us to the poor, neglected altos. In example 4.3 the altos are singing the fifth of the chord, but as we will discuss in Chapter 5, this note can easily be replaced by a note a whole-step up (the 13th in a dominant seventh chord). Listen to the difference in the sound of this harmony when the altos move up to the 13th:

EXAMPLE 4.4

The harmony becomes more challenging as we now have the interval of a major seventh between the baritone and alto parts. Less experienced singers will tend to make perfect fifths out of tritones and octaves out of major sevenths!

After the ensemble is comfortable singing this vertical structure, try raising it by half-steps. When the ensemble can confidently sing the chord by ascending half steps, add the following rhythm and have the singers snap their fingers on beats two and four.

Finally, combine this rhythm with the vertical structure as it descends by half steps:

That's how a vocal jazz ensemble like Take 6 achieves its characteristic sound! I daresay that once an ensemble understands and can successfully navigate these exercises, they will be hooked on vocal jazz forever! Listen to track 10 on the **CD** to hear the entire process.

MUSICAL ABILITIES

(For a comprehensive guide on evaluating and selecting literature see Appendix II: Music Review and Evaluation Form on page 104). There is no substitute for thorough research and score preparation prior to the first rehearsal. Once you develop the ability to get the music off the page and into your head, your rehearsal technique will instantly become more efficient. In order for this to happen, you must:

1 • Know the score thoroughly

2 • Determine the kind of sound that is appropriate

3 • Be able to quickly and effectively identify and correct errors

4 • Develop efficient and concise communication skills

The ability to familiarize yourself with the vertical and horizontal structures of each piece by hearing them at the keyboard ensures your ability to quickly identify errors.

In my own preparation of a new score, I play each individual choral part on the piano to anticipate places that will present problems or challenges for the singers, and work out possible solutions. Problem areas could include difficult intervalic relationships, extremes in range or tessitura, or harmonic/aural challenges presented by the tonal relationship of one choral part to the other choral parts. If chord symbols are not already printed in the score, I write them in prior to rehearsal. I have found this to be a valuable aid in rehearsal as well as being the best means of detecting possible publishing errors. As a writer, even though I do my best to avoid publishing errors, I can assure you, they do exist! I believe that *minimally,* functional keyboard skills are a necessity for the conductor. The ability to familiarize yourself with the vertical and horizontal structures of each piece by hearing them at the keyboard ensures your ability to quickly identify errors. The next step is to develop the ability to efficiently make appropriate modifications and communicate these adjustments to the ensemble, either verbally or non-verbally, in the least amount of time possible.

PERSONAL CHARACTERISTICS (TALK LESS, SING MORE...)

I have found that some choral directors can be verbally inclined. To put it another way, they love the sound of their own voice. To be a bit less polite, they talk too much in their rehearsals! It has been said that the best and most efficient combination for a successful rehearsal is 80% performance and 20% instruction. One of the best ways to refine your rehearsal technique and improve your efficiency is to talk less. Remember: the success of your choir's performance is predicated upon the total number of times that they have correctly and consistently sung any given piece of music. Here is an example of a rehearsal with too much "directorspeak" as well as several other scenarios that I have observed, with suggestions for improvement:

Scene 1. Fred Funkmeister would like to communicate to the ensemble a crescendo from measure four to measure eight. He says, "Okay, stop singing. Stop singing. Okay, now, you need to do that section again, okay, and this time you need to sing a better crescendo between measures four and eight, okay, so start at four and gradually get louder until measure eight so that you will be able to show better dynamic contrasts and also because there is a crescendo marking in the music between measures four and eight. Okay?" Please send that sentence to the Department of Redundancy Department! Simply put, the same information could be communicated more efficiently by either not saying anything and using conducting gestures to convey the crescendo, or by simply saying, "Thank you. One more time please, with a better crescendo at measure four" And please eliminate the "Okays." Okay?

Scene 2. A particularly challenging section of a piece is rehearsed over and over, each time with mistakes. Finally, after multiple attempts, the ensemble gives a credible reading of the section. The director says, "good" and immediately proceeds to another piece of music. The problem here is that even though the ensemble has just sung the challenging section reasonably well, it was sung well just one time. If indeed it was sung with mistakes nine times immediately preceding the "good" one, then the ensemble's consistency rate is one out of 10, and nobody likes those odds! In fact, the ensemble really spent 90% more rehearsal time singing the passage incorrectly than they did singing it correctly.

Generally, I am pleased with my ensemble's singing when they achieve the 80-90% consistency range. Therefore, in the challenging sections, we make many repetitions, each time emphasizing a new and different musical element. On each successive pass I might say:

"Good. This time, listen harder for the balance."

"This time, let's think about the dynamics."

"Very good, but your sound needs more smile."

"Sing that and snap your fingers on two and four at the same time."

After several run-throughs, many of the technical difficulties and musical problems solve themselves through simple repetition, and the overall confidence of the ensemble improves. When the ensemble has sung the phrase one time really well, use that as a point of departure to sing the phrase at least as well three to five more times

Remember: the success of your choir's performance is predicated upon the total number of times that they have correctly and consistently sung any given piece of music.

in a row. This rehearsal technique reinforces the positive aspects of the music making process and greatly enhances the ensemble's confidence through consistency.

Scene 3. Betty Bebop has the choir sing a selection that still needs rehearsal. Upon completion of the piece, she offers the choir a litany of corrections: "Tenors were flat at measure 32, everyone cut off on beat three in measure 16, altos are too loud at four after the coda, tenors were still flat at 48, sopranos, as usual, you were perfect, basses…oh, never mind. Okay, put that away and take out…"

The only way you can be sure that your ensemble knows a piece of music is by hearing them perform it well consistently.

Although these suggestions might be valid, the problem is that in spite of the fact that the conductor pointed out the areas in need of improvement, the ensemble never sang them. So Betty was wasting her breath as well as rehearsal time, and the ensemble had no chance to improve. Remember: The only way you can be sure that your ensemble knows a piece of music is by hearing them perform it well consistently. By consistently, I mean three to five times in a row in one rehearsal, then at least once more later in the rehearsal to see if the information was retained. Then, revisit the same material at the next rehearsal to see how much was retained from day to day.

Scene 4. Cathy Contrapuntal has a lovely singing voice and uses it to illustrate how a vocal line or phrase should sound. She then proceeds to sing along with the ensemble on each successive run through, sometimes creating a solo sound that can be heard over the entire ensemble. Although imitation and sonic modeling can be excellent teaching methods, I believe it is impossible to hear your ensemble when you are singing an individual line at the same time. In order to be prepared to make suggestions for improvement, you must be able to hear all parts of the choir without any extraneous influences, especially your own voice! Also, you need to give the choir the opportunity to hear themselves without you helping.

The following suggestions are perhaps not revolutionary, but they are methods that can help make your rehearsals more efficient and enable your group to sound better.

1 • Begin a new piece by rehearsing the most challenging part of the score first. This way, the singers will have lived with the hardest part the longest, and what could have been a major challenge has become second nature. Conversely, it is a waste of time to keep singing easier parts of the chart, as the ensemble will sing those well with very little rehearsal time.

2 • Rehearse a piece from the back to the front. That way, when the ensemble arrives at the end of their first read-through, the ending will be familiar and there can be a huge psychological lift when that occurs.

3 • Create a positive rehearsal attitude. The ensemble needs to know that their rehearsal time is sacred, and that they are expected to give their best effort from the start to the finish of every rehearsal.

4 • Have a rehearsal plan. You should know what you intend to accomplish for each rehearsal, and how you will achieve this. Your plan should include the specific sections of each piece you intend to focus on, and how much time you will spend on each piece. The concept of real time is something that eludes many directors. For a piece of music that lasts three minutes in performance, there will be hours and hours of time that is spent in the

rehearsal and preparation process. As a result, it is important to have an idea of the real time that will go into the learning process for each composition you program.

All that being said, keep in mind that even the best-laid plans do not always work. We have all experienced rehearsals where the entire ensemble is on the same wavelength, and they are soaking up everything musical happening. And of course there are those rehearsals that make you think aliens abducted your entire group and replaced them all with their evil twins. In either of these situations, don't be afraid to toss out your lesson and go with "Plan B." Flexibility is an essential ingredient on the path that leads to rehearsal bliss.

5 · Anticipate where the musical problems will be in every piece of music and determine the most efficient way to solve the problem. Typically, we will listen to and rehearse an individual line until the singers have learned their part with a degree of confidence and consistency. However, many times the individual line is not the cause of the problem, but instead, HOW that line relates to some or all of the other parts. Therefore, it is good to work repetitions in the following ways:

- All parts *a cappella* individually, start slowly and work up to tempo

- Men's parts alone

- Women's parts alone

- Outside parts (soprano and bass)

- Inside parts (alto and tenor)

- Build chords and lines from the bottom up, adding one part at a time

- Build from the top down, adding one part at a time

- Add rhythm section instruments when appropriate, starting with bass, then piano, then drums

6 · Connect the last chord from a previous phrase to the initial chord of a new phrase. A frequently overlooked problem is the vocal, tonal and technical adjustment singers must make from phrase to phrase. Typically we tend to rehearse starting at the beginning of a phrase. In fact, it is more efficient to start at the end of the previous phrase so that the singers can gain confidence in connecting the sections of any piece of music. It is also good to repeatedly move back and forth between two challenging chords or phrases, once again ensuring confidence and consistency in the singers.

7 · Bring energy and intensity to your rehearsal. Singers respond to a fast-paced, energetic rehearsal. If you bring genuine excitement and enthusiasm to every piece you program (and the literature you select is of high quality), you will not have to convince your singers that they are singing good music. Your actions will speak louder than words! If you are excited, your singers will be excited. Use your imagination to inspire your singers and always insist on 110% effort from the ensemble. Strive for excellence and do not

settle for anything less. Over time, your singers will rise to whatever level of expectation you establish for them.

8 • Singing is a mental and physical exercise. Keep your singers' minds engaged in the rehearsal, using intensity, pacing and focus. Do not give your singers the opportunity to lose their focus or become distracted. Once you achieve discipline, intensity and focus consistently in rehearsal, these wonderful attributes will be easily transferred to performance.

9 • Teach performance aspects such as facial expression, memorization, physical presence, and stage attitude in the rehearsal. These important elements will not magically appear in concert; they need to be emphasized and reinforced on a regular basis.

Remember to be patient. The development of an ensemble takes time and a commitment from you and the ensemble members. Because we live in a society that emphasizes instant gratification, many of your students will expect results overnight — even though they may have little experience with the concepts required to achieve and sustain musical excellence in the vocal jazz area. They might complain initially, but ultimately your students will thank you for your high expectations. Do not lower your standards to accommodate the inexperienced or developing ensemble. Keep your eye on the sky and insist that that your students continue to rise to your level of expectation.

Finally, this chapter is called *Rehearsal Techniques for the Vocal Jazz Ensemble: How Do They Differ From Traditional Concepts?* I am sure by now you have realized that, in fact, there really are no essential differences between the vocal jazz ensemble rehearsal and the concert choir rehearsal. Every rehearsal technique and suggestion listed in this chapter is applicable to any ensemble, regardless of style or genre. I assume the same persona in rehearsals and apply the same rehearsal techniques to vocal jazz ensembles, concert choirs and instrumental groups with equal success. It is my hope that you will aspire to and achieve new, higher levels of music making through a concentrated study of rehearsal efficiency. Have fun and enjoy the process!

CHAPTER 5
Jazz Theory (in Reality!)

One of my favorite expressions in the jazz theory course that I teach is, "Everything you were taught in theory is not necessarily true in reality — at the very least, it doesn't always apply." Some of the Baroque era theory rules I'm referring to include:

1 • Parallel fifths between voices are not allowed when writing choral music

2 • Roots and fifths are the most important parts of any chord

3 • Beats one and three are the most important beats in common time

4 • The chord progression of IV-V-I is the most common cadence

5 • Chords are usually constructed using thirds and sixths

And the list goes on.

Theory class has traditionally been something that most music majors either fear or loathe. Actually, when explained well, theory can not only be fun, but can also have many wonderful, practical applications to real music! To use the foreign language analogy, theory is a language unto itself, which, if practiced on a regular basis, can become a useful means of expression. Jazz musicians depend on their knowledge of theory when thinking about forms, chord progressions, chord voicings, key relationships, improvisation, arranging and composition. Although this chapter is not intended as a textbook for jazz theory, some basic concepts will be covered that will increase your theory **HQ** and provide some practical tools that should prove to be useful. (Please refer to the Appendix IV: References on page 116 for a list of jazz theory books.)

Jazz musicians depend on their knowledge of theory when thinking about forms, chord progressions, chord voicings, key relationships, improvisation, arranging and composition.

WARM-UPS

An excellent way to incorporate a theory lesson into your choir rehearsal is through the warm-up. Many directors and ensembles use the same, simple choral warm-up exercises on a daily basis, such as 1-3-5-3-1 on a specific vowel and syllable modulating by semi-tones (example 5.1). Although these kinds of exercises are useful for warming up the voice, the student's intellect, ears, and sense of ensemble are seldom challenged.

One logical first step in developing your ensemble's theory chops is to expand this type of warm-up to include minor, diminished and augmented triads as well as major, minor, whole tone and chromatic scales:

ALSO TRY THESE EXERCISES USING "SCAT" SYLABLES LIKE "DO BAH" OR "DO BEE"

The next step is to move to minor seventh and dominant chords:

Using the minor and dominant warm up exercises together can be an excellent way to get your singers comfortable with the all-important ii7-V7-I progression:

After developing your ensemble's ability to sing these new vocal exercises, not only will their voices be sufficiently warmed up; their pitch accuracy, aural skills and theory knowledge will also be greatly enhanced. Listen to tracks 11, 12, and 13 on the CD to hear how effective these warm ups can be with a vocal jazz group.

BASIC CHORD VOICINGS

In jazz, we commonly deal with music that comes from a lead sheet:

The first time I saw you, I knew that must be true, and I thanked my luck-y stars

The chord symbols above the melody are a system of shorthand that has developed over the years through common practice to represent the changing harmonies. The concept of voicings (i.e., the specific notes that a pianist, guitarist, arranger or composer chooses to create her/his desired sound) is a flexible one, whereby factors such as range, texture and inversion will ultimately determine how a specific chord sounds. What follows is a basic example of chord symbols commonly found on a jazz or pop lead sheet and the most basic voicing for each chord.

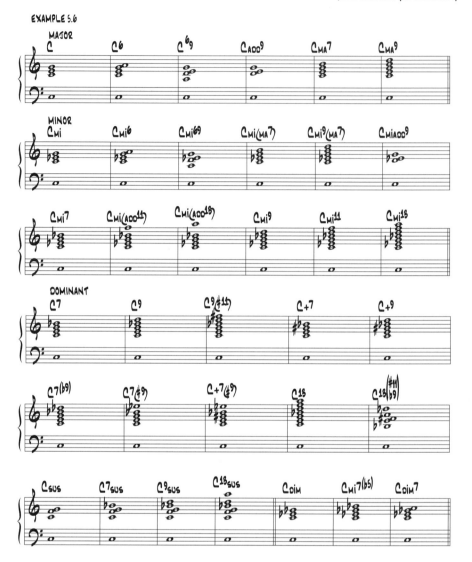

BASIC KEYBOARD VOICINGS

There are basically three qualities of chords: major, minor and dominant. In jazz theory, we often hear of the chord progression ii7-V7-I (as shown in example 5.5). This progression is probably the most common in jazz and popular music. In a major key, these chords will have the following qualities:

- ii – minor

- V7 – dominant

- I – major

Therefore, the three basic qualities are covered in this common chord progression. It is important to remember that there are only 12 different keys on the piano, therefore only 12 different major, minor and dominant chords. Once a student has learned those 12 keys and those 12 chords in each quality, there are no more new chords to learn! What is left to learn is how to use voicing to make chords flow smoothly in a progression. The following example is an illustration of this using two notes in the right hand (the third and seventh) with the root in the left hand.

EXAMPLE 5.7

As I'm sure you remember from your theory classes, the third and seventh (not the root and fifth!) are the most important notes in any chord because they determine the harmonic quality of a chord. This example also shows how music in this style violates the stacked thirds idea of chord construction. Part of what makes chords sound "jazzy" is the use of anything except thirds when voicing a chord. Once this exercise is mastered through all the keys, any pianist (yes, even you!) will have a much easier time reading and comping from a set of chord changes.

Since the Baroque era we have become accustomed to four part musical texture as evidenced by string quartets and **SATB** choral writing. In jazz harmony, we also tend to use four part structures as the basis for harmony. In a jazz ensemble, there are typically four trumpet parts, four trombone parts, and four saxophone parts (as the fifth saxophone is often doubling another part). The following is an example of good, basic, 4-note piano voicings for a ii-V7-I progression in the keys of C, B♭ and A♭. These voicings can be used as a basis for writing or arranging choral parts for the vocal jazz ensemble.

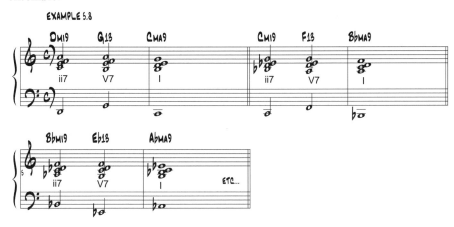

EXAMPLE 5.8

ALTERATIONS

One of the most important devices that composers and arrangers use to add harmonic interest to traditional harmony is chord alteration. Using these alterations and extensions wisely can make the difference between a vanilla sounding piece and one that sparkles. Example 5.9 illustrates a basic guide to the possible alterations, and how to voice them.

- Major chords (1,3,5,7) can add 9, ♯11, or 6 (or 13)

- Minor chords (1, ♭3, 5, ♭7) can add 9, 11 or 6 (or 13)

- Dominant chords (1,3,5, ♭7). This is where the most alterations (and combinations) occur. Here are the four 4 possible alterations to a dominant chord:

- ◆ ♭9   ◆ ♯11 (or b5)

- ◆ ♯9   ◆ ♭13 (or +5)

Common combinations of alterations to the dominant include:

- ♯9 ♯5 (♭13 ♯9)

- ♭13, ♭9

- ♭9 ♭5 (♯11 ♭9)

EXAMPLE 5.9

MAJOR ————————————————————   MINOR ————————————————————
CMA9   C⁶⁹   CMA9(♯11)   CMI9   CMI7SUS   CMI6/9

DOMINANT (THIS IS WHERE THE MOST ALTERATIONS ARE POSSIBLE) ————————————————
C7(♯9)   C7(♭9)   C13   C13(♯11)   C+7(♯9)   C13(♭9/♭5)   C7SUS

ETC....

BASIC FORMS

There are several common jazz song forms that will be useful for you to know as you select and rehearse music with your ensemble. The two most important forms are the blues and the thirty-two measure song.

The blues is usually a twelve bar form that can range from harmonic simplicity to harmonic sophistication. Example 5.10 is a traditional blues in its most basic form.

♪ EXAMPLE 5.10

The same form is typically modified harmonically in the following way when played and sung by jazz musicians. Again, notice that the harmony is outlined perfectly using only the third and seventh in the right hand, root in the left hand.

EXAMPLE 5.11

By adding a four-note voicing and basic rhythm in the right hand (I refer to this as the "Charleston" rhythm, based on the dance that was popular in the 1920's) and a walking bass line in the left hand, you can develop your ability to play the blues with minimal practice. I suggest learning this progression in the keys of F and B♭, as they are the most typical keys used in jazz music and will be appropriate for most vocal ranges.

♪ EXAMPLE 5.12

The 32-bar song is the other very common form found in jazz, popular music and Broadway repertoire. George Gershwin's *I Got Rhythm,* Jerome Kern's *Smoke Gets In Your Eyes,* and the Duke Ellington/Billy Strayhorn tune *Satin Doll* are all excellent examples of the 32 bar **AABA** form. The **A** section is an eight-measure phrase that is repeated. The eight-measure **B** section, referred to as the bridge or release, usually moves to a different tonal center and presents contrasting material. The **A** section is then repeated a third and final time.

Many songs have been composed using the chord changes from *I Got Rhythm* (usually referred to as "rhythm changes"), so it is very useful to have these chords under your fingers:

♪ EXAMPLE 5.13 ("RHYTHM" CHANGES)

Some other possibilities using a 32 bar form are: **ABAC** (*All of Me, But Beautiful, Long Ago and Far Away*), **ABAB** (*A Foggy Day* using a four-bar tag), **ABCA** (*My Shining Hour*) and **AABC** (*Robbin's Nest*).

I realize that the prospect of learning all these chord progressions and theory concepts can initially be overwhelming, but, like all other aspects of music-making, if practiced on a regular basis, they will ultimately become a vital part of your musical vocabulary. You will have a new set of tools that will help in the learning, comprehension and appreciation of vocal jazz arrangements. These concepts will also greatly assist you in the teaching process, and can serve as the basis for you to start arranging vocal and instrumental music. You can make sure that your students have the knowledge to communicate efficiently and intelligently with any musician they encounter, and gain instant credibility because of their knowledge. With these lofty aspirations as your goal, it should become your mission to develop a basic working knowledge of jazz theory, and, as a result, help contribute to making the world a bit more of a musically intelligent place. So, what are you waiting for? Start practicing those ii-V7-I's!

CHAPTER 6

The Rhythm Section

So many drummers,
so little time...

There is no substitute for live instrumental accompaniment for the vocal jazz ensemble. Just as it is important for instrumental conductors to develop enough knowledge to relate well to a vocal ensemble, it is equally important for choral directors to be able to communicate and relate well to an instrumental ensemble. "Choral musicians are from Venus, drummers are from Mars" might be a way to describe the feelings of many teachers I have encountered. Fear not! Almost all drummers have feelings just like the rest of us. And all the instrumentalists *want* to do really well in your ensemble. They simply need direction and specific suggestions. Gaining the knowledge you need to communicate effectively with your rhythm section is within your grasp. From an educational and philosophical perspective, it is important to emphasize that the vocal group and the rhythm section are two equal components that must work together to create a sense of ensemble. All too often there exists a scenario that pits the rhythm section against the singers. This situation is counterproductive to the music-making process and needs to be avoided.

There is no substitute for live instrumental accompaniment for the vocal jazz ensemble.

The rhythm section usually includes some or all of the following instruments; piano, synthesizer, bass (electric and/or acoustic), guitar, drums, and auxiliary percussion. In Gold Company, I also include a horn section that consists of two trumpets, tenor saxophone and trombone as an integral part of my instrumental ensemble. Each instrument in the rhythm section has a unique, important function and each contributes its own sounds, rhythms, colors, and textures to the musicality of the ensemble. Remember that keeping time for the vocal ensemble is not the exclusive responsibility of the rhythm section. The ability to count and maintain a constant tempo is also the responsibility of each singer. The members of the rhythm section will be challenged to do the following:

- Play the music in the appropriate style

- Read the chart and play specific rhythms, harmonies or melodies where written

- Play with great feel in a constant tempo

- Watch the director and each other

- Maintain appropriate dynamic balance within the section and with the vocal ensemble

- Play with great energy, intensity and dynamic contrasts.

That's all!

I often ask members of my rhythm section, "How many drummers are in this ensemble?" "How many bass players?" "How many pianists?" The players need to be reminded that they are one on a part, so their personal musicianship plays a significant role in the overall success of the ensemble. This thought can often motivate rhythm players to prepare their music, practice it and bring their best attitude to the rehearsal.

I realize there are conditions that exist that make live instrumental accompaniment difficult or impossible. If you have limited instrumentalists, here are several ways to allocate your forces:

- Piano alone

- Piano, bass (acoustic or electric)

- Piano, synth (covering the bass part)

- Piano, bass (or synth), drums

If rehearsing and performing with a rhythm section is out of the question, accompaniment tapes and CD's are available for many choral publications, but please use these only as a last resort.

PIANO

Writing now as a pianist, it pains me to say that unless the piano is the only accompaniment instrument, it is not the most important component of the rhythm section. (Can you guess which instrument is? Read on...) The role of the pianist in vocal jazz is usually quite different than the role of accompanist in the concert choir. The piano in the vocal jazz ensemble provides harmonic, rhythmic and melodic support. The responsibilities of the pianist in the vocal jazz ensemble can include the following:

- Playing the written piano part when necessary

- Playing the vocal parts of the arrangement

- Playing appropriate rhythms to help define the style of music

- Playing short melodic or harmonic "fills" where there are open spaces in the vocal score

- "Comping" (jazz lingo for reading chord changes) behind soloists and unison parts in the vocal score (see Chapter 5, pages 30-32 for more information and some basic jazz piano chord voicings)

- Playing improvised solos when appropriate or when indicated in the score.

Many vocal jazz charts have written piano accompaniments that work very well. In my published choral arrangements, I make it a point to write a piano part, which, if read literally, will sound like jazz. I do this specifically with the non-jazz pianist in mind. This way, all pianists who can read music can also learn to play the harmonies and rhythms that we generally associate with the jazz style. In this situation, it is the responsibility of the pianist to practice what is written and take care to realize the musical details of the score including correct notes, rhythms, dynamics, fingerings, phrasing and articulations.

BASS

The bass is the most important member of the rhythm section (if you guessed "the bass" you win the prize!), and in fact, of the entire vocal/instrumental ensemble. The bass player has two primary functions:

1 • The bass provides the harmonic foundation for the music. In many vocal

jazz charts the root of the chord is not written in the vocal parts, so the bass essentially becomes a fifth voice, frequently playing the root of the chord. This allows much more flexibility for the composer/arranger when making note choices in the four vocal parts. This is why it is vitally important for the singers to be able to hear the bass player, and for the bass player to play in tune.

2 • The bass establishes the sense of time, rhythmic pulse, and groove for the entire ensemble. As a result, it is important that the bass player learn to play with an absolutely constant tempo. Many people assume the drummer has the primary responsibility of keeping time. While playing with a constant tempo is certainly a necessity for the drummer, the bass player is truly the heartbeat and focal point of the contemporary rhythm section. The bass player and drummer must be sensitive to and hear what the other person is playing, so that these two players can lock in with a unified sense of tempo.

The ideal instrument for the vocal jazz ensemble is the upright double bass (sometimes referred to as the acoustic bass). The electric bass is also acceptable and can function perfectly well within the vocal jazz ensemble. In fact, the electric bass is sometimes preferable for pieces in contemporary pop, rock and funk styles. However, if a bass student has serious intentions in music, he/she must learn the double bass (and arco technique) to be accepted in most college and university music programs.

Both the double bass and electric bass are usually played through an amplifier, and sometimes also through the monitor and main speakers. So the bass player must know how to play the instrument and how to "play" the amplifier. It is quite common for bass players to adjust their amplifiers and tone on subsequent pieces, especially when the style changes.

The bass player must know how to play the instrument and how to "play" the amplifier.

In swing style, it is best to have a clear, well-defined tone that is easily heard by the performers and the audience. Generally this means adding brightness, clarity and treble, especially on songs with a faster tempo. A darker sound with more mid-range and bass is more common on slower tempo songs and in rock or pop styles. However, the bassist should take care to avoid too much low end in the sound as pitch definition becomes lost. I realize that it seems like an oxymoron to suggest less bass sound on the bass instrument, but that is typically what must happen. Feel free to experiment with the sound from the amplifier and the sound through the main and monitor speakers. Keep in mind that different performance sites will probably call for tone and volume adjustments for all of the instrumentalists. Ultimately, your own ears will be the best guide for your musical decisions. The bass player also must trust you to decide what is the appropriate volume from the instrument, the amplifier and the sound system. Many times the sound and volume that the bass player hears is substantially different than what the singers and audience hears.

Other important considerations for the bass player:

• Always tune the bass to the piano prior to the performance! The piano is a fixed-pitch instrument, so all other instruments need to adjust to the keyboard.

• To help get a well-defined bass sound, the bass amplifier should be elevated off the floor. Use a speaker stand or sturdy chair.

- The bass player must learn how to play even quarter notes in a walking bass line. A slight accent on beats two and four will help the swing feel. This is not an easy task and must be practiced before it can be mastered.

- The player should connect the sound of one note to the next. To do this, the bassist should keep her/his fingers on the string at all times, even while shifting positions. While pressure on the string can be released, do not remove the fingers from the string during shifts.

- Realize that the tone of the instrument can be altered, depending upon where the string is pulled in relation to the bridge of the instrument. Playing closer to the bridge creates a brighter sound that may be appropriate for rock, pop and funk styles, while playing farther up on the neck will produce a more mellow sound. Learn to pull as much sound as possible from the bass. The amplifier should serve only to amplify the sound of the acoustic instrument, but the fullness and richness of the sound should emanate from the instrument itself.

- The double bass has four strings. Electric basses are made with four, five or more strings, and can be fretted or fretless. Each type of electric bass has advantages and disadvantages. It is a personal decision of the player as to which instrument works best. But remember: there is no substitute for the double bass!

I realize that it may be impossible for some vocal jazz directors to have a bass player in the ensemble. If this is the case, you must remember that the bass part is a crucial ingredient in the vocal jazz ensemble. Most synthesizers have a good acoustic string bass setting. A keyboard bass played through an amplifier is the next best thing if a real bass is not available. Anyone with competent keyboard skills can learn to play the bass line. As a last resort, the bass part can be played on the low end of the piano, but remember, that would be your *last* resort!

HOW TO CREATE A "WALKING" BASS LINE

A bass player who is not familiar with the jazz idiom and has little experience reading chord changes can follow these three rules to create competent and acceptable bass lines:

1 • In the swing style in $\frac{4}{4}$ time, play the root of the chord on beat one, the fifth on beat two, and the root on beat three

2 • Approach changing harmonies (usually on beat one and three) by a note a half step above or below the new chord tone

3 • For variety, use stepwise motion in the scale of whatever chord is written

EXAMPLE 6.1

DRUMS

Pity the poor drummer. Most often they are subjected to the same, repeated mantra that is *not* music to their ears: "You're playing too loud!" In fact, one of the most overlooked aspects of the drum set is that it is a musical instrument capable of huge dynamic contrasts. The drum set, in the hands of a competent player, can offer a full palette of colors and a wide variety of sounds. The drummer has the function of orchestrating the ensemble, while playing with a constant tempo. The first responsibility of the drummer is to lock up with the bass player and establish a constant tempo in the correct style of the music, and then to groove hard! Once a great groove is established, the drummer can begin to explore her/his creativity and add colors and effects that contribute to the overall musicality of the ensemble. Although the ability to play a constant tempo is one of the primary responsibilities of the drummer, they do not have sole responsibility for maintaining the underlying time of the ensemble. Each singer and player must contribute to the unified sense of time.

The drum set, in the hands of a competent player, can offer a full palette of colors and a wide variety of sounds.

We can draw an analogy between drum equipment and automobiles. When considering the purchase of a new automobile there are many important factors to consider, some of which include budget, model, options, and size. There are so many choices that the task can be daunting. The same myriad choices apply to drum sets as well. However, the drum set (also referred to as a "kit") most often preferred by jazz drummers is a simple, basic set that consists of cymbals and drums. Here are some of the important details:

Cymbals. This may come as a surprise to you, but in many ways the cymbals are the most important part of a jazz drum set. The **LCD** includes a pair of hi-hat cymbals, a ride cymbal, and perhaps one or two others. Of course, you might have seen the barrage of cymbals many rock drummers include in their set up. Usually this represents a severe case of overkill and way too much hardware on the stage. Although it looks impressive, there is no musical need for too many cymbals. (Perhaps this is where the term "heavy metal" actually comes from!) Here is an explanation of what cymbals are required in a basic drum kit:

Hi-Hat Cymbals. Usually 13 or 14 inches in diameter, medium to medium-thin weight. The hi-hat is the pair of cymbals that open and close and are played with the left foot. This (along with the ride cymbal) is one of the most important pieces in the kit. In swing the hi-hat cymbals open and close to create the distinctive "chick" sound on beats two and four. This is one of the most important aspects of good time keeping, and is essential to the style.

Ride cymbal. Usually 18 to 22 inches in diameter, medium or medium-thin weight. The width and weight of each cymbal determines the sound of that instrument. Every cymbal really does have a different and unique sound. Once again, the taste and preference of the player (and you) will determine which cymbals to play. The ride cymbal is usually played with the right hand and provides the famous "spang, spang-a-lang" ( ) sound that is so prevalent in swing jazz.

Other cymbals. Three other cymbals typically found in a jazz drum set are the crash/ride cymbal, the splash cymbal and the sizzle cymbal. The crash/ride is usually 16 to 18 inches in diameter and medium-thin or thin weight. This cymbal is used for accents, fills, or as an alternate ride cymbal when variety or contrast is required. The splash cymbal is typically smaller, usually 8 to 10 inches in diameter and thin weight. This is an excellent cymbal for accents. Another commonly used auxiliary ride cymbal is the sizzle ride, which has rivets in it. This gives a more sustained sound that can be particularly effective on ballads.

Drums

Bass Drum. Typically 14 or 16 inches deep with an 18 or 20-inch diameter. A 20-inch bass drum is more versatile and perhaps more appropriate for vocal jazz ensembles that often incorporate a wide variety of musical styles in their programs. The 18-inch bass drum is used more by straight-ahead jazz and be-bop players and may be too confining for a vocal jazz ensemble. The bass drum, also referred to as the kick, is played with the right foot. There are differing opinions as to when and how much the bass drum should be played. In swing style, I believe in playing the bass drum very lightly on all four beats and also in using the drum sparingly, primarily for support, punctuation and accents.

Snare Drum. Typically $5\frac{1}{2}$ or $6\frac{1}{2}$ inches deep by 14 inches with either a wood or metal shell. There is a lever on the side of almost all snare drums that engages the snares (under the drum). This versatile drum is most often played with the left hand with the snares "on." In latin music, the snare is usually off which gives the drum a small tom-tom sound. The snare drum is used to play fills, to set-up and accent rhythmic figures in the vocal parts, and to provide a strong back beat. The back beat happens on beats two and four and should be emphasized in jazz, rock, pop, funk and gospel styles. Another common snare drum technique is to use a drum stick crossed over the drum and played on the rim. This sound can be particularly effective in latin style music.

Other drums. In the basic jazz drum set, two more drums are typically used. The ride tom, placed over the bass drum, is typically 8 or 10 by 12 inches and the floor tom is usually 14 by 14 inches. These tom-tom drums are typically used for fills, accents, and are also very effective for latin beats.

Each drum should be tuned differently, so that the depth of tone in each drum increases as the dimensions of the drum increases. The tuning should be open, with a round, full tone. The bass drum should be lightly muffled to give definition to the sound while retaining a full tone. The snare drum is often muffled with an "O" ring to give added clarity and a deep, full sound.

There are two basic configurations of drum kits that would be ideal for the vocal jazz ensemble:

1 • Four-piece kit: 14-inch snare drum, 10-inch mounted tom, 14-inch floor tom, 20-inch bass drum

2 • Five-piece kit: 14-inch snare, 10 and 12-inch mounted toms, 14-inch floor tom, 20-inch bass drum

The jazz drum set generally is smaller and lighter than its rock counterpart. Good things *can* come in small packages! The jazz drummer will take great pride in her/his ability to create a wide variety of sounds and grooves from the minimum amount of drums and cymbals.

Other important considerations for the drummer:

- The drummer should own and know how to use sticks, brushes, and mallets. The drum sticks should be made of lightweight wood (not the Lincoln log variety favored by rock drummers!) with wood tips. Brushes are often used on ballads, or to change timbres. Mallets are the same as those used to play marimba, and when used on a cymbal can create a beautiful crescendo.

- Be aware of dynamic contrasts. However, never confuse dynamics with intensity. The drummer should always play with great energy and intensity, regardless of style and volume.

- Drummers need to learn to read music, and especially learn how to read jazz charts. In the vocal jazz ensemble rhythm section, the drummer should be very familiar with the vocal parts so that they can make intelligent, musical contributions in rehearsals and performances.

The drummer needs to be sensitive to the amount of sound generated from the instrument, and make sure they are not overplaying, or playing too loudly. However, when a drummer is playing in a vocal jazz ensemble in which the singers are on individual microphones, the level of sound can be higher, and in fact, can resemble big band playing. The singers will not need to oversing because of the amplification of the sound system, and the audience will be treated to a highly energized, exciting overall musical presentation.

Finally, the drummer is a musician first, who happens to play the drums. The drummer needs to think of herself or himself as a musician, and needs to be treated as a musician by others. Of course, one must earn this status. But if great art were easy, everyone would do it!

If great art were easy, everyone would do it!

Example 6.3 demonstrates three different styles of music played on a standard five-piece jazz kit. It is important to note that drum parts can be notated in a variety of ways ranging from the very general "swing for 8 bars" to very specific written parts for each drum and cymbal of the set. The examples in 6.3 give the drummer enough information to accompany the ensemble without being cluttered — make sure that your drummer has a part that looks something like these examples.

♪ EXAMPLE 6.3 (THREE DRUM STYLES)

GUITAR

In the rhythm section, the role of the guitar is similar to the piano. The guitar can provide harmonic, rhythmic and melodic support to the ensemble. Comping should also be familiar to the guitarist. The player must learn appropriate voicings for all chords and the appropriate rhythms to play for various styles. Also, the guitarist can provide a single-line melody that can either double voice or piano parts. Of course, the guitarist can also be an additional featured soloist.

The jazz guitarist probably will have different equipment than the rock guitarist. The jazz guitar sound is typically warmer and less harsh than a rock guitar sound. Because the guitar is usually played through an amplifier, the guitarist needs to know how to control the tone functions on the instrument, as well as those on the amplifier in order to achieve the ideal and appropriate sound for the vocal jazz ensemble. This sound could vary from song to song, depending on style and the forces being used. It is also imperative to play with dynamic sensitivity and achieve proper balance within the rhythm section and within the entire ensemble.

The guitar must always tune to the piano or the fixed pitch keyboard instrument. This should be done *before* the concert, or before the first piece is performed. Because the guitar and piano perform similar functions in the rhythm section, it is important to define responsibilities for each instrument. Each piece of music needs to be discussed and a specific plan formulated for the pianist and guitarist. They need to coordinate the specific voicings used to make sure the chords have the same quality and the same extensions.

Each piece of music needs to be discussed and a specific plan formulated for the pianist and guitarist.

For comping, the two players must make sure they do not step on each other by playing too much and at the same time, thereby cluttering the music. Example 6.4 from *One in a Million* (track 19 on the **CD**) illustrates how busy a rhythm section can sound when both the guitar and piano are comping without a plan and without listening to each other.

♪ EXAMPLE 6.4 AND 6.5 (ONE IN A MILLION)

In straight-ahead swing charts the standard style of guitar comping is called "Freddie Green." Named for the great guitarist from the Count Basie Orchestra, this style calls for the guitar player to use down strokes on each quarter note. By slightly releasing the pressure in the left hand after each stroke and slightly accenting beats two and four, the guitarist will achieve the distinctive sound associated with this style. Now, the guitar, bass and drums all "line up" rhythmically, and the piano player has more freedom for short fills and solos. Listen again to the same segment of *One in a Million* to hear how this sounds.

By the way, it is relatively easy to make the transition from electric guitar to the electric bass. I am aware of many excellent double bass players in jazz who began their musical experience by playing rock guitar. After discovering the limitations of the rock idiom, they raised their **HQ** a few points, moved to jazz guitar, then experimented with electric bass, and finally made the move to double bass. This is a logical, and, relatively speaking, easy transition to make. If there is more than one guitarist in your program, you should encourage them to play the bass guitar. As an incentive, you might mention that there are *way* too many guitarists in the world, and never enough bassists. If the player becomes competent, she/he will *always* have a gig and be in demand, and, as a result, have the opportunity to make lots and lots of money. I have found that this last bit of information can be particularly motivating for some younger musicians!

AUXILIARY PERCUSSION

Often an ensemble will have the luxury of more than one drum set player. If this is the case, encourage your students to develop their abilities on other percussion instruments. These include: conga drums, timbales, tambourine, cow bell, shakers, claves, bell trees, wind chimes and African or South American instruments. The percussion players can then alternate on various pieces of music, which will increase the versatility of each player. As is the case with the pianist and the guitarist, the drummer and percussionist must "get on the same page" regarding who is playing exactly what, and when they are playing it! When the two players are well coordinated, auxiliary percussion can add a wonderful variety of colors, rhythmic excitement and intensity to the ensemble. As always, you must use your own best judgement and good taste to determine what is appropriate on each song. Percussion is most typically added on pieces written in the latin style, but also can be effective additions to pieces in the rock, pop, funk and gospel styles.

Another way to add the colors of percussion instruments to the performance is to have singers in the ensemble play them. The singers will need to be taught the correct technique for each instrument, and they must practice singing and playing at the same time. This task may sound easier to accomplish than it actually is. Make sure the singers have many opportunities in rehearsal to develop confidence in playing the percussion instrument. It would be unfair to the student and the ensemble to expect them to expertly play a new instrument on very short notice. It is also a recipe for potential disaster in the performance.

CONCLUSION

Finally, I am amazed at the number of rhythm sections that I encounter who completely disregard the necessity of a proper physical set up. Example 6.8 illustrates a standard rhythm section set up that works well with a vocal jazz group.

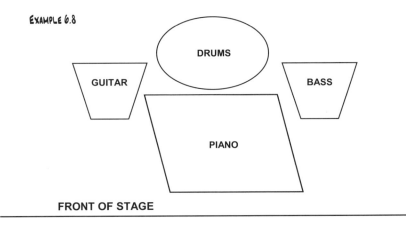

EXAMPLE 6.8

The location and proximity of one player to the other is extremely important. The rhythm section players must be able to establish visual contact with each other. It seems that some less experienced players somehow (erroneously) get the idea that it is cool not to look at each other while playing. In fact, the players with the highest **HQ**'s insist on being able to see each other. Also, the players need to hear each other, and, more importantly, need to be able to listen to each other. In order to do this; each player must practice their individual part until they own the material. I suggest that each rhythm section member play their part from memory. Once the players commit the score (either the specific notes or the chord changes) to memory, they will have more available brain space for musical input and will be able to listen to each other much better. As a result, there will be more musical interaction, and the overall level of performance will improve significantly.

CHAPTER 7

The Art Of Solo Singing

Singing a solo in the contemporary idiom, whether jazz or pop, is a style, art and craft unto itself. Many vocal jazz ensemble charts require a soloist to step forward and perform, and we often expect inexperienced (and usually petrified) singers to deliver a solo with all of the confidence of a professional. We need to take the time, as does the soloist, to make sure that solo passages are as well rehearsed as the ensemble sections of any given piece.

There are significant differences between jazz singing and pop singing. Although both jazz and pop singing have specific stylistic requirements, generally the jazz singer's focus is on creative note choices, thoughtful delivery of the text, improvisation, and artistic statement. Most often, a jazz singer chooses to sing jazz because it represents a fresh, unique and creative form of musical expression. They sing jazz simply because they *have* to! If the jazz singer is able to ultimately earn money by singing jazz, that's a bonus. On the other hand, the pop singer is often motivated by more commercial influences. Pop music usually has a wider audience and is generally less sophisticated than jazz. For all solo singing however, I suggest the student study voice to develop a healthy technique, then learn to apply that good technique to whatever style they choose to sing. I am a strong advocate of versatility of style and tonal flexibility. Ultimately, the singer who has a flexible and versatile instrument will be more marketable and more likely to find employment as a singer.

One of the most intriguing aspects of solo singing is that every person has a unique voice. Just like fingerprints, there are no two voices that are exactly the same. And one of the best aspects of jazz singing is that it doesn't necessarily require a "beautiful" (by Western European classical standards) voice to be successful. The singing voices of Ella Fitzgerald and Louis Armstrong were never destined for an operatic career, yet these jazz singers had an important and profound influence on those who followed. Every singer — regardless of voice quality — has the potential to make an original musical statement.

The solo jazz singer experiences myriad intellectual, technical, and musical challenges that, when successfully mastered, will result in an artistic and creative statement. The goal of the aspiring jazz singer is to make a unique sound and develop a personal and individual interpretation of any song. As in classical music, there is an immense volume of great jazz literature that is available for the aspiring jazz soloist to listen to, study, and perform; more than can possibly be known well in a lifetime. Therefore, the jazz singer can always look forward to discovering and learning new repertoire. Improvisation is another crucial ingredient in the recipe for great jazz singing. The range of improvisation can run the gamut from a simple alteration of the written melody to harmonically, rhythmically, and melodically sophisticated scat singing. Finally, the solo jazz singer is faced with the multiple challenges of being able to sing songs that are performed at a constant tempo with or without rhythm section in a variety of styles, and sing ballads at a very slow tempo usually using rubato.

The following recommendations apply to songs performed at a constant tempo, regardless of style:

1 • The soloist must develop a sense of jazz phrasing. The most common form of jazz phrasing is "back phrasing," or singing behind the beat. This technique, commonly used by jazz and pop singers, involves singing the melody and lyrics later in the measure than they are written. The rhythm section or accompanists play the song using a constant tempo while the vocal soloist delays the placement of the original melody.

One of the best ways to learn this technique is to listen analytically to singers who use back phrasing effectively. I believe that listening to great artists is by far the best method to achieve familiarity and sophistication in solo singing. Frank Sinatra, Tony Bennett, Ella Fitzgerald and Sarah Vaughan are four singers with highly accessible styles, who have mastered singing behind the beat. Their interpretations sound effortless, but when you try to sing along with them, word for word, note for note, breath for breath and phrase for phrase, you will discover that this technique is not as easy as it sounds. One of the best effects of singing behind the beat is the tension or anticipation that is created within the listener. As a result, the performance becomes more interesting and more compelling.

In example 7.1, jazz vocalist Sunny Wilkinson demonstrates a strict rhythmic rendering of *But Beautiful* and then a step by step process showing how a singer can transform and personalize the same phrase.

♪ EXAMPLE 7.1

Music by Jimmy Van Heusen Words by Johnny Burke
Copyright © 1947 (Renewed) by Onyx Music Corporation (ASCAP) and Bourne Co.
All rights to Onyx Music Corporation administered by Music Sales Corporation (ASCAP)
International Copyright Secured. All Rights Reserved.
Reprinted by permission.

The opposite of back phrasing is "front phrasing" where the singer places notes, lyrics and rhythms ahead of the place in the measure they are written. Even though this device is found much less often than back phrasing, there are situations where it can be used effectively. Jazz singer Mark Murphy and Brazilian singer Joaó Gilberto provide masterful models of front phrasing.

2 • The original melody and rhythms are simply guidelines and may be interpreted and altered to create a unique statement. *It is necessary to learn and memorize the original melody and lyrics during the initial stages of studying a new song.* Once this original information can be sung with confidence, encourage the soloist to experiment by altering the melody and rhythm (using back phrasing or other techniques) in order to personalize the song (see Chapter 3, page 8). This process stimulates creativity and is enjoyable and liberating. The individuality of expression that comes as a result of this exercise can be wonderfully rewarding and satisfying for the singer. Tremendous artistry can be achieved either by mastering the original melody

It is necessary to learn and memorize the original melody and lyrics during the initial stages of studying a new song.

and lyric, and honoring the songwriter's original material, or by taking that material to an entirely new place through improvisation and alteration of the original melody, harmony and style.

3 • The singer must feel a subdivision of the rhythm and tempo. In straight ahead $\frac{4}{4}$ jazz this subdivision is swinging eighth notes; in $\frac{12}{8}$, it is the triplet; in most latin grooves, it is the even eighth pulse with emphasis on beats two and four, and in Afro-Cuban salsa music, the clave (either 2+3 or 3+2) is the subdivision. This feeling must be developed and practiced until it becomes second nature. Refer to Chapter 3 for detailed information on these grooves.

4 • Generally, in faster tempos, the rhythm should be felt more on top of the beat. In medium and slower tempos, the groove can be more laid back.

5 • Use classical or choral breathing technique and inhale and release in tempo.

BALLAD SINGING

Ballad singing is one of the most challenging musical experiences facing a solo singer.

Ballad singing is one of the most challenging musical experiences facing a solo singer. A certain maturity, poise, and confidence is required of the singer. In ballads, the soloist should:

1 • Sing the lyrics in an almost conversational manner. The lyrics must be learned, memorized and practiced literally as poetry. Explore which words or syllables should receive more emphasis, and the duration and pitch that will be assigned to each syllable. This is one of the best methods of developing a personal interpretation of a song. Determining the important words in a phrase and emphasizing them (in duration and pitch), while de-emphasizing the words not vital to the idea expressed by the text will make the best interpretive use of the lyricist's words.

2 • Many standard songs were written with a verse that precedes the more familiar chorus or refrain. Singers often overlook these verses, but it can be very effective to perform the verse using a speech-like delivery of the text in a moving rubato tempo. This concept is analogous to the tradition of recita-tive and aria commonly found in classical music. Again, Sinatra is a good model. He would often include the verse to *I Get a Kick Out of You*, *I've Got a Crush on You* and *Where or When*. Also, singers almost always include the verse when performing *Lush Life* and *Dindi*.

3 • Create an appropriate emotional mood that reflects the text (happy, sad, angry, humorous, reflective, nonchalant, etc.) As in all singing, a certain amount of theatricality will help convey the message of the text.

4 • Although improvisation is less common (though certainly acceptable) in ballads, changing and ornamenting the written melody will add interest and personalize the song.

5 • Use space. It is okay to *not* sing! The soloist must learn to feel comfortable when not singing and to enjoy silence and rests in the interpretation of a ballad. For two excellent examples listen to Ernestine Anderson sing *Georgia on My Mind*

on her album with Ray Brown *Live at the Concord Jazz Festival* or listen to any Shirley Horn ballad interpretation.

6 • Use dynamic contrasts to help reinforce the text.

7 • Use your own imagination and creativity when considering how a ballad might be performed. Interest can be created through the use of variety of forces. For example, the soloist could start an **AABA** song by singing the first **A** section a cappella, then adding bass on the second **A**, and then bringing in the rest of the rhythm section at the bridge. Another effective method to achieve variety in a ballad is to create a double time feel for a portion of the song, perhaps in sections where improvisation occurs.

THOUGHTS ON PRESENTATION

Make sure that your students understand and are comfortable with these ideas, whether they are performing as an individual singer or as a soloist from within the group:

- Wear attire that is appropriate for the performance venue.

- Hold the microphone slightly below your mouth and face in a relaxed, comfortable position. Experiment with each microphone you use to find the placement that gives the best amplified recreation of your voice.

- Get enough rehearsal time on the sound system to be able to develop a body language and stage presence that exudes confidence. Your stage attitude and emotional state should reflect the message of the text.

- Establish a line of communication with the audience. I encourage singers to keep their eyes open when they sing. Although singing with the eyes closed may be an effective temporary dramatic device, remind them that the eyes are the most expressive part of their face.

- Practice any dialogue that you have; speak clearly and intelligibly.

- Use diction that is in the vernacular and is easily understood.

The art and craft of solo singing is one of the most challenging and ultimately rewarding experiences a singer can undertake. There exists a virtually insurmountable volume of literature that musicians can draw upon as a source for developing their individual skills, creativity, musicianship and intellect. Regardless of their age or experience, you can encourage your singers to take a chance and experiment with this fun and exciting idiom. The musical rewards and artistic satisfaction that can be experienced will justify all of the hard work and effort that they put into their personal and musical development.

The art and craft of solo singing is one of the most challenging and ultimately rewarding experiences a singer can undertake.

MUSIC LITERACY AND THE SINGER

I know that you might find this hard to believe, but occasionally in the world of instrumentalists there is a less than positive attitude toward singers. One of the biggest challenges facing the developing jazz singer is the ability to work with and relate to their instrumental accompanists. The root of this schism is most often found in musical background and competence. It is not enough for a singer to know just the name of a song that they want to sing; they must also know the key, tempo and form of the piece. Let us explore two student musicians:

1 • Student **A** begins taking piano lessons in the second grade, learning music fundamentals and theory. In the fifth grade she begins to play trumpet in the school band. She first must learn to produce a sound on her instrument and develop the appropriate technical ability required. After six years in the concert band the student is now in high school and has attained a high degree of proficiency on her instrument. She performs in concert band, marching band, and jazz band. She participates in solo and ensemble competitions and summer music camps. By the time she reaches college age, our student is ready to be a music major. She has been playing trumpet for seven years, has developed sight-reading and music theory skills, and has basic keyboard competencies. This has been accomplished over a period of several years that included regular, disciplined practice, ensemble participation, and technical study.

Compare this scenario to Student **B**.

Disclaimer: It is important to note that Student **B** is a (mostly) fictitious character and that many singers are serious about their musical studies thanks to the tireless efforts of the dedicated teachers and conductors with whom they study (that's you and me)!

2 • Student B never showed much aptitude toward music during his elementary years. His interests ranged from sports to sports. In his junior year of high school he needed an elective course and was placed (against his will) in choir. As it turns out, when he opened his mouth to sing, there emerged a lovely baritone voice that was surrounded by leading man looks! The fact that he had no knowledge of music theory and could not read music was secondary to the fact that he was a baritone with a lovely natural voice who could sing in tune and be a featured soloist in the fall choir concert. Add his good looks and natural athleticism to the equation and the star of the high school musical production is born. All of his choral music was taught to him by rote and his emerging natural talent and developing ear were the only tools he needed to achieve success at this level.

The following year he decides to audition for college as a voice major. He still can't read a note of music, but the beauty of his voice earns him a large scholarship because the college *needs* baritones. Even though he studied voice privately in college, he seldom practiced for his lessons, learning his music by rote (from his accompanist), continuing to gain success due to the natural beauty of his voice. In spite of his lack of knowledge and discipline regarding music, he found himself one day singing on the Broadway stage, where he made lots and lots of money, and was taught all of his roles by rote. Everyone knew he was a functional illiterate when it came to music, but it did not matter, because of the beauty of his voice.

The differences in musical skills between Students **A** and **B** should be obvious. The point is that there need to be some "dues" that are paid when developing one's musical abilities. These dues include regular, disciplined practice over an extended period of time, study, technical development, listening, music theory, history, and styles. And the dues are even more challenging for the jazz musician, because they must develop skills in improvisation, an entirely separate discipline unto itself. Gone are the days when a singer can simply open up their mouth and sing. It is imperative that all singers make every effort to become educated musicians. I am usually annoyed and amused when I hear the phrase "singers and musicians" used in the same sentence to describe two different genres of people! In fact, with the availability of jazz programs, audio and video recordings, and publications throughout the world, there is no excuse for all singers not to become competent, educated musicians. Additionally, singers should also be familiar with the basic components of composing and arranging.

Please refer to Appendix III: For the Aspiring Soloist on page 108 which includes some thoughts and ideas written with a student musician in mind.

It takes time,
patience and
determination
to do anything
worthwhile well.

CHAPTER 8

Improvisation

Jazz improvisation will not be covered in great detail in this book. It is an area that is too extensive to examine thoroughly in one chapter. There are a number of wonderful resources available to assist students and teachers interested in developing their jazz chops — several of these are listed in Appendix IV: References on page 116.

Improvisation is one of the most important elements in jazz performance. It is also one of the most challenging, and is something that can strike fear and panic in even the most accomplished musicians! The fact that improvisation is now found almost exclusively in the jazz idiom is ironic. Historically, improvisation was an essential and integral part of the classical music tradition. Improvisational elements were found both in vocal (plainchant and organum) and instrumental (court and folk music) idioms in the Middle Ages. Music of the Renaissance and Baroque eras was full of improvisation. In fact, figured bass, a staple of Baroque era compositional techniques, was intended as a purely improvisational element. Individual composers throughout history were acclaimed for their improvisational abilities as performers. J.S. Bach was capable of improvising four and five voice organ fugues, a musical and intellectual feat that I find truly awesome. Haydn, Mozart and Beethoven would regularly improvise the cadenzas in their piano concerti. In the Romantic era, Chopin, Liszt and Brahms were known for their virtuosic improvisatory abilities. It was only in the 20th century that improvisation became essentially non-existent in the classical world. There are many classical musicians today, however, especially organists, who are capable of improvising.

"Scat singing" is the
term used to describe
vocal improvisation.

"Scat singing" is the term used to describe vocal improvisation. In the most traditional sense, singers attach nonsense syllables (shoo, be, do, yah, bop, dah, bah, bo, di-dle-ee, etc.) to their improvised pitches. Scat singing developed in the 1930's and 40's when singers used their voices to imitate improvised lines and phrases played by jazz instrumentalists. The great jazz innovator Louis Armstrong made one of the first well-known recordings of scat singing in 1926 on a song entitled *Heebie Jeebies*. According to legend, the lyric sheet fell to the floor during the recording session and Armstrong was forced to sing nonsense syllables because he didn't know the words! When you hear recordings of his singing, it is obvious that his vocal improvisations are simply an extension of his trumpet playing.

I also find it ironic that scat singing developed from vocalists' attempts to imitate jazz instrumentalists. In the late 19th century, instrumental jazz pioneers often learned to play their newly acquired instruments without regard to the traditional methods of playing the instrument. Their technique and sound may have been "wrong" by Western European classical standards, but their playing was vibrant and alive. At that point, they were imitating vocal styles and effects to create many of the elements of a new instrumental jazz style. When the early scat singers then imitated the styles and inflections of the horn players, we had come full circle!

Perhaps the best and most succinct definition of improvisation is spontaneous composition. Conversely, music composition could perhaps be best described as improvisation done very slowly: one note at a time! In either case there is a craft and a discipline involved in the process. One of the best analogies to describe the process of learning the improvisatory language is to compare it to the process of learning a foreign language. For example, if you study French in high school and college, you could, over time, develop the ability to speak and write the language. However, even though you would have a functional knowledge of the language through academic study, you would most likely speak French with an American accent and in a proper, non-conversational manner. If you wanted to master the language, you would go to France and spend an extended period of time there, immersed in the language and the culture. The subtleties of the language, the slang, the vernacular and even the accent could then become second nature for you. The same immersion applies to vocal and instrumental improvisation.

The most common language of jazz scat vocabulary is rooted in the bebop era of the 1940's and 50's. This era is widely known as the "common practice period" in jazz because historically, most of the jazz that has followed contains stylistic elements derived from bebop. Just as a student of French needs to expose their ears to the sound of the French language, a serious student of jazz improvisation must become immersed in the sounds, styles and inflections of bebop over a long period of time. It is important to emphasize that ultimately improvisational skills will be directly related to the amount of time invested in quality practice and listening.

Just as a student of French needs to expose their ears to the sound of the French language, a serious student of jazz improvisation must become immersed in the sounds, styles and inflections of bebop over a long period of time.

Example 8.1 (from *Doctor Blues*) is a transcription of an improvised instrumental line in the bebop tradition. Listen to how the soloist uses scat syllables to imitate the phrasing and articulation of the saxophone soloist.

♪ EXAMPLE 8.1

(DOCTOR BLUES, MEASURE 45)

bu-du-la doo doo da dah___ doo doo dah dah dah doo de doo de dah dah dot

bu did-dl-y dah bah doo dah___ did-dl-y doo bah___ bah bah bah___ doo___bah doo wee___

bah did-dl-y doo daht dah___ doo dee doo bah doo bah doo bee doo bee daht doo dah___

did-dl-y doo bee doo dah___ boo dah bah doo bee doo dah___ doo bee dah doo bee

did-dl-y doo bee dah___ did-dl-y doo bee dah___

Example 8.2 (from *This Masquerade* track 23 on the **CD**) illustrates how scat syllables can be used with a newly composed melody over an existing set of chord changes.

This is an excellent way to begin to understand the process of improvisation.

Here are several exercises that I recommend to students who demonstrate an interest in developing their improvisational abilities:

1 • *Listen, listen, listen to improvised jazz.* Naturally it is important to be familiar with vocal jazz improvisers. These include Ella Fitzgerald, Sarah Vaughan, Mel Tormé, Bobby McFerrin, Betty Carter, Darmon Meader, Mark Murphy, Dave Lambert, Jon Hendricks, Carmen McRae, Michele Weir, Kevin Mahogany and Kurt Elling as well as many others. It is just as important to know some of the major instrumental soloists as well. Miles Davis, John Coltrane, Charlie Parker, Thelonious Monk, Dizzy Gillespie, Sonny Rollins and Stan Getz are all excellent examples.

2 • *Transcribe recorded solos.* The best approach to this project is to select one

recording and listen to it repeatedly until the student can accurately notate the pitches and rhythms on staff paper. Then, with the original chord changes written over the improvised solo, compare the newly transcribed melody with the original melody of the song. Study and analyze the specific note choices of the original artist and then practice singing the solo with the recording, imitating every pitch, phrase, breath and articulation. If a written transcription is not possible, then an aural one will also assist in absorbing the scat vocabulary. Imitation is one of the very best methods of learning to improvise.

3 • *Extract one or two melodic phrases* from the transcribed solo, preferably a melody that is sung or played over a ii-V7-I chord progression. Learn to sing this phrase with pitch accuracy and jazz articulations in all 12 tonal centers.

4 • *Pitch accuracy* is one of the most challenging aspects of developing scat singing technique, especially on pieces with a faster tempo. Learn a specific phrase by singing it very slowly and reinforcing the pitches at the piano. Then gradually increase the tempo without sacrificing the ability to maintain a consistent tonal center.

Over the years I have been blessed with many talented vocal improvisers in Gold Company. The characteristics these singers all shared include:

- the ability to spontaneously select and vocalize notes that are compatible with the underlying harmonies
- the ability to sing in tune and with accurate pitch
- the use of a variety of syllables, articulations and vocal effects that imitate instrumental jazz
- the development of a jazz vocabulary based on the bebop language
- study of music theory so a thorough knowledge of the relationship of scales and chords is developed
- the development of (at least minimal) keyboard skills
- a passion for listening to a wide variety of vocally and instrumentally improvised jazz
- the ability to imitate and mimic the specific vocal sounds from recordings
- the ability to understand and follow the form and phrase structure of the music as well as the ability to hear and anticipate chord changes
- the ability to interact with members of the rhythm section
- the bravery and confidence to step forward and take a chance on singing a solo, even if it was scary or challenging

If you have access to the recordings made by Gold Company (see Appendix I: Vocal Jazz Discography on page 91), you can hear these young students in the earliest developmental stages of their careers as creative improvisers. I can attest to the fact that these students are not any different (mentally, physically, emotionally or musically) than most students found anywhere. Also, usually they are not highly developed scat singers when they enter our program. They simply have an intense desire to improve their abilities, and more importantly, practice their craft regularly and repeatedly.

Finally, I do not consider myself a great teacher of scat singing, nor does it occupy a large part of my rehearsal time. All of my students are required to improvise, and those who make scat singing practice a part of their regular routine invariably develop into improvisers who would make any teacher proud!

CHAPTER 9

The Sound Reinforcement System

There is a part of me that would love to ignore anything having to do with technology and electronics. But to do so would be to ignore one of the most important aspects of music today. The fact is, sound amplification, microphones, speakers, synthesizers and computers are here to stay. We must come to this realization and embrace new technology. Not only will we find growth and improvement in our ensembles and ourselves, we may even have some fun and learn something in the process! George Bernard Shaw said, "Progress is impossible without change; and those who cannot change their minds cannot change anything."

I have developed a healthy love-hate relationship with all aspects of technology. There are many times while directing a vocal jazz ensemble that I long for the technical simplicity of directing a concert choir. I can also remember the "good ol' days": a time when sophisticated sound systems were not necessary or required for vocal jazz. But, like hoop skirts, the Edsel and 8-track tape players, that time no longer exists! Consider that not long ago voice mail, cell phones, email and "dot com" were not a regular part of our lives or our vocabulary; I rest my case!

Although there is no absolute right or wrong regarding sound systems, I am a firm believer in using a sound system for the vocal jazz ensemble.

Although there is no absolute right or wrong regarding sound systems, I am a firm believer in using a sound system for the vocal jazz ensemble. Specifically, I believe the best form of amplification is a multiple-microphone system with as few singers as possible on each microphone. There are numerous reasons to try to avoid sound systems, including expense, maintenance and setup/teardown time. But for every reason to *not* use a sound system, there are several important justifications in favor of it.

First of all, each singer is challenged to achieve the best possible pitch, blend, intonation and balance when singing close to a microphone. Their voice cannot hide — it must achieve musical and sonic equality with the other singers. Ultimately, this will help you set higher standards for your students in these areas. Second, the vocal instrument will be preserved. When using a microphone properly, the singer avoids the risk of vocal strain that results from oversinging. Too often, performers are asked to "sing louder" in an attempt to be heard in a large gym or auditorium or when singing with instrumental accompaniment. Using a quality sound system allows a good sonic balance to be achieved and eliminates the singer's need to shout or needlessly push the voice. Third, contemporary technology includes sophisticated microphones and sound systems; they are used in all aspects of professional music. This technology is here to stay... so we are doing a disservice to our students if we do not teach them about proper microphone technique and sound reinforcement. Also, a sound system can allow you to achieve a balanced ensemble sound with unbalanced vocal forces. A group with 12 women and four men can sound like a balanced **SATB** vocal ensemble! Also, a younger male voice with a limited lower range (not unlike mine!) can help the sound of the bass section by singing softly, with accurate pitch, very close to the microphone.

For me, one of the most wonderfully frustrating and ultimately satisfying aspects of rehearsing an ensemble on a sound system is the challenge of achieving a great choral sound while taking full advantage of all that sound reinforcement technology has to offer. As a teacher, you will experience tremendous musical challenges and growth as you establish higher standards for your students in the areas of blend, balance and intonation.

Clearly, for many choral directors, the sound system is one of the most problematic areas within the vocal jazz idiom. There are many traditionally trained choral musicians who are philosophically opposed to the artificial enhancement of the acoustic sound of the human voice. It is important to emphasize that the sound system does not magically make your ensemble sound better. On the contrary, close mic singing will expose every wart that exists in your ensemble sound. Whenever I am in a workshop or clinic with Gold Company singing, I always eagerly anticipate the skeptic in the audience who will ask, "They sound good *on* the system, but how do they sound *without* microphones?" The questioner assumes that the sound system automatically improves and enhances the sound of the ensemble, and that without the microphones the ensemble will not sound as good. In fact (much to the dismay of the skeptic), the ensemble sounds exactly the same off the microphones, just not as loud!

Before we look at the five basic hardware components of a vocal jazz sound system, there are two general ideas that you need to consider before spending any money. First, I suggest that you buy the very best components possible for your entire sound system, even if you have to spread your purchases out over several years. Remember that you are investing in the sound of your ensemble and that this is an investment in equipment that should last for at least ten years. Secondly, if you have access to a local retail store that specializes in **PA** equipment, I urge you to establish a relationship with an audio specialist there instead of buying on-line or through a mail-order catalog. Even if you pay a few dollars more for the product, the peace of mind you will have knowing that help and service are available on short notice will be priceless. You just never know when something might blow up — but it is probably a safe bet that it will be at your final dress rehearsal!

Buy the very best components possible for your entire sound system, even if you have to spread your purchases out over several years.

MICROPHONES

Audio people often refer to "signal flow." This term indicates the direction that the sound or signal is moving through the sound system. So the signal flow in a vocal group begins with the singers and the microphones. As mentioned earlier, the ideal situation in a vocal jazz ensemble is an individual microphone for each singer. There are several types of microphones designed for various purposes.

The *dynamic* microphone is probably the best choice for vocal groups. These mics are cost effective and rugged so they can withstand the constant use and abuse that set up, tear down and travel can have on equipment. They also produce a warmer sound than other types of microphones, which is very effective with a choral group.

Another choice is the *condenser* microphone. These mics have greater high-end clarity than the dynamic microphone, but they are more fragile and usually require an additional battery or external power source, referred to as "phantom power." It is common to find condenser mics in recording studios where there is less wear and tear on the equipment.

As your sound system becomes more sophisticated, *wireless mics* will also be an option. The great feature of these microphones is that they allow performers total freedom of movement without any hassling with cables. In Gold Company, we typically use dynamic mics for the group vocals with two or three condenser mics for the soloists.

Another consideration when purchasing microphones is the pick-up pattern. This pattern describes the optimum area of sound source that the mic will cover. Since it is best to isolate each singer's voice as much as possible, the *unidirectional* pick-up pattern is best if you will have only one or two singers very close to each mic (figure 9.1). However, if you decide to have three to four singers around a mic, the better choice is an *omnidirectional microphone* (figure 9.2). The major drawback of an omnidirectional mic is that they pick up sound from all sides, so when you turn up one of these mics all the extraneous sound is amplified along with the singers.

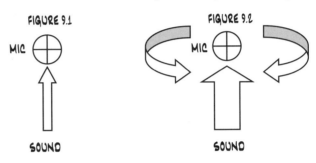

When purchasing microphones, ask the salesperson to set up a comparison with different microphones running through the same sound system.

When purchasing microphones, ask the salesperson to set up a comparison with different microphones running through the same sound system. By hearing your own voice through that system, you will be able to determine the differences in sound generated by different microphones. Also, take a male and female singer from your group with you to the store to get a clear idea of how your singers sound with various microphones. You will immediately hear how different microphones create different sounds, even when all other factors are equal.

One final factor that you should consider when purchasing microphones is *impedance*. Low impedance (Low-**Z**) microphones are a much better choice for the vocal jazz ensemble because they can be used with microphone cables longer than fifteen feet. Although high impedance (High-**Z**) microphones have higher output and are often less expensive than Low-**Z** microphones, they are far less practical for most vocal jazz because the shorter cables they use severely limits the movement of the singers. There is also considerable loss of high frequency response and the possibility of unwanted hum and noise.

SOUNDBOARD OR MIXER

This piece of equipment is designed to receive and balance all of the sound coming from the microphones. Each microphone will plug into a separate input on the soundboard and each of these inputs will have separate controls for volume (or gain), equalization (**EQ**), reverb, effects and monitor level. It is best to purchase a soundboard with as many inputs as possible, but at the very least you should have sixteen.

The ideal location for the soundboard (and audio engineer) is in the middle or in the back of the concert hall. It is best to locate the soundboard slightly off center to avoid adjusting the choir's sound in the "cancellation zone": the area where the sounds from the left and right speakers meet. This placement will allow the audio engineer to hear what the audience is hearing, and to adjust the overall sound during the performance accordingly. Placement of the sound board to the side of the stage or backstage is not a good idea because the audio engineer will have no idea how the ensemble sounds through the main speakers.

You will also need a *snake*, which is a group of microphone cables bundled together that serve as the extension cord that runs from the stage to the soundboard. The snake is a neat and clean way to transfer the signal from the microphones to the soundboard.

AMPLIFIERS

Amplifiers are the power source that drives the main speakers and the monitor speakers. The signal originates from the microphone, runs through the soundboard and then to the input of the amplifier. The amplifier then powers the signal and sends it through the speakers. The amount of power in an amplifier is measured by the number of watts per channel; somewhere between 1800 and 3400 watts should be sufficient for a vocal jazz ensemble. Units with this amount of power will allow your ensemble to be heard in larger auditoriums and gymnasiums and will decrease the chances of sound distortion. Generally, one amplifier is designed to drive from two to six speakers. Again, this is where the help of an audio specialist is invaluable because they can match your amplifiers to your speakers to guarantee that there will be enough power to operate your system.

SPEAKERS

The main speakers are the primary source of sound that your audiences will hear. Remember that your ensemble will lose its "acoustic" sound, and that the audience will be hearing the sound of your ensemble as it originates from the main speakers, not directly from the stage. Because of this important fact, it is necessary to select a speaker that gives excellent reproduction of the voice from the bottom of the range to the top. Typically, these cabinets will include one or two 12 to 18-inch speakers, one to two 6 to 8-inch speakers, and a small horn (or tweeter) which will add clarity and definition to the sound, especially with the voices. Contrary to what some people might tell you, size does not matter when it comes to selecting speakers. There are some excellent speakers available which produce a sound that is clearly better than models twice their size.

The main speakers are the primary source of sound that your audiences will hear.

As with microphones, the best way to hear differences in speakers is to have a set up with several kinds of speakers running through the same sound system. Perhaps your audio specialist might even be willing to set up a few pairs of different speakers in your normal rehearsal or performance space so that you can hear how the speakers sound where they will be used most often. One final suggestion concerning speakers: select a CD that you know very well to play through the speakers as you are making your decisions. This can be very helpful in determining the overall sound characteristics of various speakers.

MONITORS

Monitors are speakers that allow the performers to hear themselves during a rehearsal or performance. Good monitor sound is very important to the vocal jazz ensemble because the singers can make immediate adjustments to their blend, balance and intonation. The best speaker size combination for vocal monitors is a 12-inch woofer with a 1-inch high frequency driver or tweeter. Remember, with monitor speakers, as with the main speakers, bigger is not necessarily better. A 15-inch woofer is great for hearing low end frequencies, but is too large to respond to the fast attacks in the vocal range. The monitors should be facing the performers and turned away from the audience, making it possible to have a different sound level from the monitors than from the main speakers. Generally, I prefer the monitor volume to be as low as possible. I have found that loud monitors result in louder, unmusical singing from the ensemble. In Gold Company there are two monitors on the downstage solo mics, four more in front of the singers with two in front of each row (figure 9.3 at right). The band also has at least two monitors of their own. As a result, all the performers are able to hear each other well, which obviously contributes to the overall effectiveness of the performance.

SPECIAL EFFECTS

Of course, using a system does offer opportunities to artificially alter the sound of the group with effects such as reverb, equalization, echo, chorus, and delay. These effects are simply enhancements; they are clearly not a necessary component of your group's sound. If your budget allows, there are several of these luxury items that can give you some interesting options. These include:

Graphic equalizers. These components can be used to alter the treble and bass sound of your main and monitor speakers. Each concert hall and performance venue has unique acoustical properties and a more sophisticated **EQ** system can help create the best sound for every performance.

Effects processors. These components can electronically and artificially create special effects which can enhance the sound of the ensemble. These effects can include the addition of reverb in rooms that have little or no natural reverberation. Other effects include digital delay and echo, as well as a plethora of fun and humorous sounds that can provide interesting variety or even comic relief.

CD player. This can be connected to the sound system to play accompaniment CD's in lieu of a live band. They also are useful for providing background music for an audience prior to and following the performance.

Compressors. A compressor allows sudden and unexpected peaks and bursts of sound from vocal and instrumental microphones to be smoothed out automatically. This will help avoid distortion in the main speakers which, as we all know, creates a very unpleasant and distracting listening moment for the audience!

The only other important parts of the basic system that you will need are microphone stands. Although we also occasionally hand-hold the microphones, I prefer using mic stands because it increases the sonic consistency of the ensemble, places fewer physical demands on the singer (which may result in tension), and allows more freedom in the hands and arms for individual expression and gestures. We also use t-bars that screw onto the top of the mic stand so each stand can hold two microphones. This decreases the number of mic stands we need and creates a neater, less cluttered appearance on the stage.

If you have an ensemble that travels and offers performances on the road, it is a good idea to purchase protective cases or road boxes for all of your equipment. There are excellent cases available commercially, or they can be custom built to meet specific needs.

Ultimately, the success of your musical presentation is heavily dependent on the operation of your sound equipment and how quickly and efficiently you can set it up and take it down. Therefore, it is tremendously important to instill in your performers and crew a sense of pride in their sound system, and to teach them to handle all equipment with great care and tenderness!

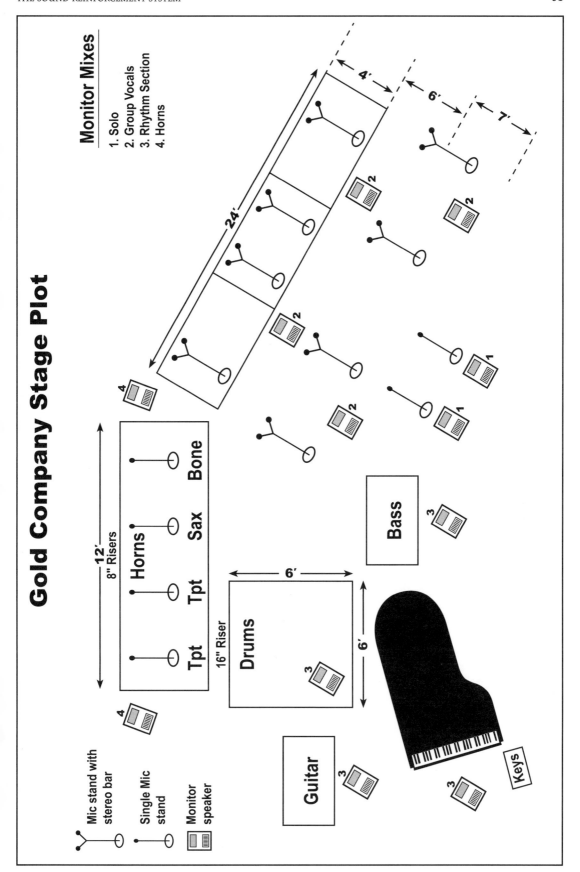

Gold Company Stage Plot

Monitor Mixes

1. Solo
2. Group Vocals
3. Rhythm Section
4. Horns

Horns

Tpt · Tpt · Sax · Bone

12'
8" Risers

16" Riser

Drums
6' · 6'

Bass

Guitar

Keys

Mic stand with stereo bar

Single Mic stand

Monitor speaker

CHAPTER 10

Staging, Movement, and Programming

I often remind my students that most audiences "listen with their eyes." We cannot escape the fact that generally, people are visually oriented. As a result, the audience at your concerts is more likely to remember what your students wore instead of what they sang! The pure musician in me finds this prospect a bit disheartening, because after the ensemble invests so much time and energy in how they sound, it seems almost inconsequential how they look. But *it isn't!* In fact, I urge you to give the visual aspect of your performance your full attention. At any type of performance, be it a musical, an opera, a stage play or a concert, when the curtain goes up, the audience reaction is usually instant. Silence, polite applause or "oohs and ahhs" express the impact of the initial visual impression immediately. And, the audience mindset for the rest of the event has also been established. We must strive to create the most positive visual impression possible and do our best to consider and connect with the audience.

Give the visual aspect of your performance your full attention.

I am one of the *least* visually inclined people you will ever meet. After an extended conversation with you, I will probably remember most, if not all, of what was discussed, but I wouldn't be able to remember what you were wearing if my life depended on it! And yet, even the "visually-observant challenged" Steve Zegree makes evaluations of an ensemble based solely on the visual aspects of a performance. Some thoughts and questions that I find myself asking include:

- Is the stage neat and clean?

- Does the set-up look professional?

- Is the stage adequately lit?

- Do the performers look like they are enjoying themselves? Are they communicating their joy in music making to the audience? Are they mentally and physically engaged in the performance? Is there energy and commitment in their presentation?

- Are the costumes or outfits neat, clean, elegant and becoming? Do they flatter the performers?

- Do the performers exhibit a sense of personal hygiene? You may think this is a joke, but believe me, it isn't!.

  From an audience member's perspective, hygiene can be demonstrated by a neat, clean and well-groomed personal appearance. From a performer's perspective, it is courteous for each performer to apply deodorant and brush their teeth. As a personal reminder to my students I discuss means to prevent perspiration. The stress, tension and stage heat encountered in performances often brings on perspiration along with those unsightly stains. Frankly, this is a subject that I would prefer to avoid (even as I write this) but I know that the advice is well appreciated by student performers.

- Does the ensemble project a sense of confidence and pride on stage? Are they disciplined in their performance?

The performers need to remember that they are on stage and that an audience is viewing them. This means that at any time, someone in the audience is able to see every person on the stage. Therefore, while on stage, it is inappropriate for the performers to make adjustments to their costumes, fix their hair, or place their hands anywhere near their face. True discipline and real professionalism can manifest itself when a performer has a terrible itch on their nose, but they have the willpower not to scratch it! Also, if a performer makes a mistake during the performance they should not convey it to the audience. I realize that the performer who makes a mistake may feel embarrassed or disappointed or angry, but these emotions have no place on stage. The audience is probably unaware of many minor errors, and the performer should never "tip the hat" when something does go amiss.

These expectations of stage behavior, discipline, attitude and etiquette can and should be instilled in any group of students, regardless of age or grade level.

When your ensemble enters the stage, the audience is making split-second evaluations (both conscious and sub-conscious) of every aspect of the performance, musical and otherwise. Their minds are formulating opinions and drawing conclusions. The best way to assure that your group will create those audience "oohs and aahs" with their initial visual impression is by making sure that the answer to all the questions above is *yes*.

I remember a commercial on television that promoted a dandruff shampoo. The phrase that caught my attention was "you only have *one* chance to make a first impression." What an important message to impart to our students! It can be applied to virtually all aspects of their lives. It has been said that a performer has 45 seconds from the time she/he appears on stage to either turn on or turn off an audience. Make sure that your group knows this and uses those first 45 seconds to their advantage!

MOVEMENT

And now we come to the great debate: Shall we dance? The definitive answer to this question is (drum roll please): *maybe!*

Of course, the real answer to this question rests with you. Your philosophy and goals for the vocal jazz ensemble and how it relates to your total choral program should dictate how much or how little the group dances. To help give you a frame of reference, let me explain how I approach this with Gold Company, and share my thoughts and reasoning.

Your philosophy and goals for the vocal jazz ensemble and how it relates to your total choral program should dictate how much or how little the group dances.

First, my students generally are not dancers, nor do they really want to be. In fact, there is no dance component to the audition process for Gold Company. At the university level, students who have a primary interest in dance will major in dance or musical theatre. Most music majors are serious about developing their musical abilities and have little time to devote to developing their dance skills. The same is true for us "teacher types." Our vocation is teaching music, not dance!

In spite of the fact that my students are often choreographically-challenged, I still want them to project a confidant and energetic stage presence, and develop at least some movement skills. Consequently, Gold Company will always have at least one formally choreographed piece in our repertoire. Because we sing close to the microphones, it is important to develop a style of choreography that looks exciting, but keeps the performers close to the mic stands when they are singing. So, obviously, our most intricate choreography is reserved for instrumental breaks or other sections of music that allow some of the performers to be off the mics. All of our choreographed selections are created by students from the group who do have some dance background. This works well for us because these students are already familiar with our style and know the music very well.

In addition, we work extensively on our "look" when we perform vocal jazz literature. This look does not involve specific choreography, but instead encourages each individual to move in a way that appears free and natural. First, we focus on the face. Each performer's hair is kept away from their eyes, as the eyes and eyebrows are the most expressive part of the face. Next we work to create a natural smile. This is not as easy as it sounds! Each student must go to a mirror and find a smile that flatters their face and then memorize that specific feeling, so the smile can be turned on at any time. Having your singers develop this ability will greatly enhance the look and sound of your ensemble.

After we have mastered the smile, we concentrate on arms, hands, and legs. Our singers stand with as little tension in their body as possible, with appropriate alignment, with a relaxed neck and shoulders, but always with a look of energy and intensity. On some pieces, we mark the tempo by slightly shifting our weight from left to right. (Keep in mind that most intricate foot choreography is often lost on an audience unless it is specifically highlighted.) The arms are naturally bent at the elbows and kept loose and relaxed. Of course we snap on beats two and four during swing and jazz tunes. Even though this is simple to read, developing this look can present a challenge to many of your singers, and will take a fair amount of time to perfect — try it yourself!

Rehearsing movement in front of a mirror or video taping a rehearsal is an enormous help for any group.

Rehearsing movement in front of a mirror or video taping a rehearsal is an enormous help for any group. Often, singers do not have an accurate perception of what their faces and bodies are actually doing. A mirror or close-up video (the camera never lies!) will help performers see when they have achieved the correct movement so that they can then commit that correct feeling to muscle memory.

The goal for an individual singer in Gold Company is to sing some of the most challenging choral literature in the contemporary idiom, and make it appear to be absolutely effortless. Each singer has the freedom to move arms, hands, head and feet in whatever manner they choose, as long as it is not distracting and does not attract unnecessary attention to the individual. If we are in couple positions (either mixed or same-sex) the couple is encouraged to react, interact and have fun with each other. Even if the couple is boyfriend-girlfriend and they just had a major argument backstage, the audience better not know about their personal lives once they are onstage! Also, when an audience sees Gold Company in concert, they should have no idea about the difficulty of the repertoire. We prefer to keep that information a secret. Of course, someone in the audience who has rehearsed and sung vocal jazz will know what the ensemble has done behind the scenes and how hard they have worked to arrive at a very high level of performance.

SELECTING A CHOREOGRAPHER

If you decide to hire a choreographer to help you with a more extensive dance sequence, you need to find someone who will be able to create appropriate movement for singers that will enhance the music and overall performance. If you have never worked with a professional choreographer before, talk with teachers whose groups are well choreographed, or attend a clinic or workshop where you can meet and work with several professionals.

Here are some questions to ask a potential choreographer:

1 • *Do you begin with physical warm-ups?* Just as a vocal warm-up is necessary prior to a choral rehearsal, a thorough physical warm-up is essential before any extensive choreography session.

2 • *Do you read music?* Although there are fine choreographers who can't read music, it is often easier to work with someone who can. Not only will they be able to see how the music flows and find appropriate places for movement, but also they will be able to communicate with you concerning any cuts or other changes made to the printed score.

3 • *Can you create movement that will flatter both genders at all times?*

4 • *Will you adjust or modify your choreography if I see a need to do so?* Obviously, they are your students, and you will have the final say in all matters regarding the ensemble.

5 • *What experience do you have working with students at this level?* Trust me, the last thing you need is someone who has only worked with experienced adults, has a prima dona attitude or a harsh demeanor.

6 • *Do you create your choreography prior to the rehearsal?* No, I'm not kidding! You need to ask this question. One of my choreographer friends refers to this as *"careography"*: what happens when the choreographer is making up dance steps as they drive to your school for rehearsal.

There are several factors that I consider important and try to instill in my students who have an interest in creating and teaching choreography. The first is to study the text of the music. The lyric will often set the mood and dictate the "look" of a piece. Just as composers can use text painting to depict lyrics, choreographers can highlight aspects of the text using movement.

Second, it probably goes without saying that the movement during a piece should reflect the style and tone of the music. No matter how cool the latest **MTV** move looks, it will be inappropriate for a swing selection from the 1940's.

Along these lines, you must consider the age and maturity level of the singers. I think it is inappropriate for younger students to imitate some of the dance styles from **MTV** or other music videos.

Third, no matter what the age of your group, a useful rule of thumb in determining the amount of movement is that the smaller the ensemble, the less choreography can be used without sacrificing vocal production.

Finally, even though the majority of your audience is visually oriented, do not fall into the trap of over-choreography. Sometimes, contrasting positions for the ensemble can be just as effective. By changing the picture you can have some dramatic visual variety, as well as giving your singers a chance to hear the group from a totally new and different perspective.

A personal aside: I cannot dance. I am perhaps one of the world's most self-conscious dancers. I have always been at the piano providing the music while everyone else danced! In fact, I have never been in the cast of a musical as a singer or dancer. You already know that I cannot sing, now let it be known that I can't dance either! In spite of my inability to bust a move, I still realize the importance of imparting at least a basic skill in that area for my students, and also that it must be addressed at least on some basic level in all performing ensembles. Think of the live performances of professional vocal groups. The King's Singers, Chanticleer, The Manhattan Transfer, Take 6, The Real Group, and New York Voices all address staging and choreography as an important part of their performance. Each group has its own style, but staging, positioning, gestures, and dance moves are rehearsed prior to their performances. Often what appears to be free, natural and improvised movement is in fact completely planned and rehearsed in advance.

There is no substitute for superior music making.

Again, it is important to reiterate that, just as there are a multitude of approaches to musical styles and rehearsal techniques, there are no absolute right or wrong ways to approach choreography and staging within an ensemble. The look of an ensemble will ultimately reflect the priorities and philosophies of the director. What an awesome responsibility for you! One of the keys to having a successful vocal jazz ensemble is establishing your priorities. First of all, your group must *sound* excellent, regardless of their age level. *There is no substitute for superior music making.* Spend an appropriate amount of time addressing the appearance of your ensemble, from exactly what they wear to where they stand, to how and when they move. They need to *look* excellent, too! Whether you like it or dislike it, agree or disagree, I strongly urge you to invest the time and energy it takes to make a strong musical and visual statement with your performing ensembles.

PROGRAMMING

Directly related to the visual appeal of an ensemble is the literature they perform, and the order in which it is presented. As I reflect on my various and sundry musical influences, Fred Waring probably had the most profound impact on my thoughts regarding programming. He always gave serious consideration to the musical tastes and demographics of the audiences for whom he was performing. I consider these factors as well when programming concerts, and make every effort to present an entertaining concert, while retaining artistic and musical integrity.

I make no apologies for considering entertainment value when creating programs, regardless of style. Many times our audiences have paid money, or otherwise invested their time and resources into our performances. I believe it then becomes our obligation to think about presenting a program that will appeal to a majority of the audience. One of your goals should be for your audience to leave the concert satisfied. (They will most likely attend future concerts, and perhaps even bring their friends the next time!) In order to achieve this goal, some serious forethought must go into your selection of music and concert planning. The following may help to inspire you to program the perfect performance!

PROGRAMMING POINTS TO PONDER

1 • *Philosophy.* Pre-determine what you want to teach your ensemble and what you would like for your audience to experience.

2 • *Real time.* It is crucial that you know exactly how long each piece of music lasts, and the length of any spoken lines or non-musical activities. If you have been asked to give a concert of a specific length, make sure you adhere to that length. By all means, do not run long. There are few things worse than a self-indulgent group or soloist who does not consider real time, thus leaving an audience feeling as though they had too much.

3 • *Imagination and creativity.* Think of the number of choral concerts you have attended or conducted that began with a piece from the Renaissance era and ended with a spiritual. Although the musical content could have been excellent, the programming was probably quite predictable. Although this may be a traditional way to program repertoire, use your imagination to break with tradition and create a new and innovative way to program and present your traditional literature.

4 • *Style.* Variety is, as they say, the spice of life! Plan a program that offers a wide variety of characteristics and musical styles. The obvious styles include swing, ballad, and latin but other genres can include novelty tunes for comic relief, songs in the style of an era (1940's swing, 1950's Elvis, etc.), medleys, or cover tunes of a specific artist or group.

5 • *Tempo.* A variety of tempos is crucial to the groove! Generally, audiences respond to contrasts. Without significant contrasts in tempo, an audience will develop ear fatigue and gradually tune out the performance. Don't be afraid to check a metronome to ensure that your tempos are sufficiently contrasting during the performance.

6 • *Key relationships.* Ear fatigue can also develop from an over-exposure to the same tonal center. Be aware of the initial and final keys of your repertoire and try to ensure that a new piece also begins in a different key than the one that has just concluded.

At this point if you are thinking "Man, Zegree is sure a perfectionist about every little detail of every aspect of every performance," *you are correct!* The professionalism in a performance comes from the music making and a commitment to all the extra-musical aspects of the show.

7 • *Accompaniment.* Sonic variety can be easily achieved through changing accompaniment forces. If your ensemble includes a rhythm section and horns, consider not using the horns on some selections, or program some pieces with just piano accompaniment, and of course, include some a cappella repertoire. If you have a competent rhythm and horn section, feature them on a piece without the singers. An ideal spot to consider programming a band tune is following an a cappella ballad.

8 • *Forces.* Just as contrast can be found in the accompaniment forces, you can program a variety of vocal forces. Your repertoire should include selections that feature the entire ensemble and soloists with vocal ensemble backing.

Also, if you have an outstanding soloist or soloists, they could be given a solo spot in the program. Variety can also be achieved through specialty acts which can include vocal combos, or even an occasional non-musical act. Just make sure a sense of artistic integrity is maintained!

9 • *Vocal/Tonal approach.* The human voice is an amazingly flexible instrument capable of a wide variety of sounds. Vocal groups should alter their sound to achieve stylistic and tonal variety from one selection to the next. Classical choral literature should sound different from repertoire in the jazz, pop, and gospel styles. A choral ensemble has the potential to sound like four or five different ensembles, even though the personnel remains the same.

10 • *Segues and transitions.* This is an aspect of programming that is often overlooked. You need to plan and rehearse how to quickly and efficiently get from one piece to the next. One of my personal pet peeves as an audience member is excessive dead stage space: an inordinate amount of time taken between performed selections. A director can quicken the pace of a concert by starting the introduction of a song during the audience applause, or by repositioning the ensemble for the next selection so that when the applause is completed the ensemble is ready to begin. It is also wise to plan and rehearse all spoken lines (yours and students) to maintain the pace and flow of the show.

11 • *Costuming.* Consider a quick, simple outfit change to add visual variety to the program.

12 • *Lighting and special effects.* Although this is certainly not a crucial aspect of a performance, lighting variety can greatly enhance a program. A follow spot to highlight soloists, or an overall stage lighting change during an intimate a cappella ballad can add a lot of visual variety. Relatively simple lighting effects can add a dramatic flair.

13 • *Adaptation.* Fred Waring was fond of saying, "You paid for the music, now do what you want to it!" (With the exception of photocopying it!) Keeping in mind the importance of maintaining artistic integrity, you should have the capability of adapting the music to suit your ensemble's needs.

As directors, part of our art and craft is drawing together all the elements of a performance (music, staging, lighting, costumes and spoken dialogue) to create a program for the audience that takes them on a ride that covers the gamut of emotions and experiences, and also educates, entertains and inspires.

I view programming as one of the most important aspects of a performance and always take great care when creating a program order. As directors, part of our art and craft is drawing together all the elements of a performance (music, staging, lighting, costumes and spoken dialogue) to create a program for the audience that takes them on a ride that covers the gamut of emotions and experiences, and also educates, entertains and inspires. When done correctly, you will have your audience on their feet, wildly applauding and demanding encores instead of on their feet beating a hasty retreat.

CHAPTER 11
Listen, Listen, Listen

Have a concept of quality, know what is best and pass it along to your students.

I am reminded of the joke about the tourist who, on his first visit to New York City, asked an elderly lady he met on the street how to get to Carnegie Hall. The reply? "Practice, practice, practice!" This advice applies to all musicians who are serious about developing their technical abilities to sing and play with any degree of competence and confidence.

For jazz musicians, it is equally important to "listen, listen, listen!" It is our obligation to know what is new and fresh, and what is great and historic. We must also know, as should our students, that the best way to assimilate the jazz vocabulary is through serious listening. The concept of listening to music may be explored on many levels. For a vocal jazz educator or enthusiast, I believe it is important to be exposed to any and all vocal or instrumental jazz groups as well as solo jazz singers to develop an appreciation for jazz style, phrasing and improvisation. Unfortunately, there are relatively few professional vocal jazz groups able to maintain a career while achieving artistic and commercial success. The sad fact is that there is a limited market in terms of audiences for live performances and also for purchases of recordings. That is why it is so important for us to be supportive of the vocal jazz art form. We must buy new CD's, purchase tickets, pay cover charges, attend concerts, and spread the word on behalf of vocal jazz in order to interest more people in this wonderful music. There is so much vocal jazz artistry that exists among us that it is our responsibility to generate new audiences for this unique art form. If *we* are not radically pro-active on behalf of quality vocal music and jazz, who will be?

It is our obligation to know what is new and fresh, and what is great and historic.

If we are not radically pro-active on behalf of quality vocal music and jazz, who will be?

I don't know how I got on this giant soapbox, but as long as I'm here, please allow me one more rant! Generally speaking, the entertainment corporations that control the recording industry dictate popular musical tastes to us. It is important to remember that the recording industry is a *business* whose primary interest is to sell as many CD's as possible. That is why, throughout the history of recorded music, we have been consistently bombarded by pop music of questionable quality. Disco and rap music both come to mind. (Can you say oxymoron?!) You are in a position to influence the musical choices of your students; please use that influence to elevate their sophistication and intellect through the selection of high quality, artistic music in the jazz idiom. If enough people purchase enough copies of vocal jazz groups and solo artists, I guarantee that the record companies will produce more vocal jazz recordings.

WHAT DO WE LISTEN FOR IN VOCAL JAZZ, AND HOW DO WE DO IT?

It is important to develop your ability to critically listen to a recording. Many times we have music in our lives as a byproduct of other activities. For example, we might have the radio on in the car, or play recordings while we clean the house or exercise. In these cases, the music is secondary, and truly incidental. That is fine, but we must also learn to focus our intellect and really listen to music. This is not an easy task, and takes concentration and effort. Also, it is an activity that you should include as a regular part of your musical life. There is a vast quantity of wonderful recorded music that can serve to educate and inspire us. It would be a pity to not be exposed to it. Once you and your students have honed your abilities as world-class listeners, your knowledge, sophistication, and **HQ** will rise significantly.

A good method to develop listening skills is to select one piece from a recording and listen to that example numerous times, each time focusing your attention on a different aspect of the performance. Before you play the recording, read all of the available printed information including personnel and liner notes. It is amazing how much information can be obtained through the study of **CD** liner notes. Here are some evaluative criteria that will help you and your students focus your attention on each successive listening of your selected piece.

Listening Evaluation Form
designed by Diana Spradling

Objective Information

SONG TITLE _____

COMPOSER _____

ARRANGER _____

LYRICIST _____

PERFORMER _____

ALBUM TITLE _____

Album Information

RECORDING LABEL _____

RECORD NUMBER _____

DATE OF RECORDING SESSION _____

VOCAL AND INSTRUMENTAL PERFORMERS _____

_____

_____

_____

It may be helpful to obtain a printed copy of the original song. This can usually be found in a fake book or in the original sheet music of the song. Because much of vocal jazz is the arranger's rather than the composer's art, it is interesting to analyze how the arranger adapted the composer's original music.

FORM

Identifying the song form will help in following the structure of the recording, especially if there are improvised solos. There are many types of forms composers use in jazz and pop music (see Chapter 5, page 32 for examples and definitions).

STYLE

Once again, the arranger can take the original source material and choose to write the song in virtually any style. It can be fun and refreshing to hear a tune in a musical context that is entirely different than what we would expect. For example, an arranger might set the ballad *Here's That Rainy Day* as a bossa nova or a swing tune. Here are several style categories:

- *Swing*

- *Latin*

- *Ballad* (see chapter 3, page 8 for specific examples of the above)

- *Bebop*. A stype of Jazz that developed in the 1940's that uses intricate eighth note-based melodies with quick harmonic rhythm.

- *Cool*. A West Coast style that developed in the 1950's which followed and was perhaps a reaction to bebop. This style of music typically has a much slower harmonic rhythm and less complex melodies than bebop. Cool jazz innovators include Gerry Mulligan, Miles Davis, Paul Desmond and Stan Getz. (Please do not confuse cool jazz with today's so-called "smooth" jazz. The two styles are not related!)

- *Fusion*. A combination of rhythmic and stylistic elements from pop, jazz, rock and/or latin music.

- *Funk*. A style that incorporates elements from gospel, blues, rock and/or jazz.

- *Traditional Jazz (or TradJazz)*. New Orleans or Chicago style Dixieland. This music usually has a "front line" of trumpet, clarinet and trombone and a rhythm section that includes drums, banjo and/or piano with acoustic bass or tuba. The rhythm section feel in Dixieland is sometimes referred to as "second line."

- *Big Band*. This ensemble usually has ten or more players and performs highly arranged music. "Big band" can refer to the ensembles popular in the 1940's like those headed by Glenn Miller or Duke Ellington, or to more contemporary bands like those led by Bob Mintzer or Maria Schneider.

THE ARRANGEMENT

Are there unique introductions, transitions or endings? How does the arranger use different orchestration (a cappella, instrumental accompaniment, etc.)? Are there modulations, tempo or groove changes, rubato, wide dynamic contrasts, or other distinguishing characteristics?

THE RHYTHM SECTION

One of the best ways to learn about the function of the instruments in the rhythm section is through several repeated listenings that focus on each individual instrument. Accompaniment devices that are common include all players playing simultaneously, only one or two instruments playing while others drop out, double time feel, half time feel, and stop time. It is also interesting to hear how the solo singer or the group interacts with the rhythm section.

IMPROVISATION

Is there any improvisation? If so, is it harmonically and melodically sophisticated? Does the singer use scat syllables or words from the song or a combination of both? Do they cover a wide vocal range? How do they use breath and space? How is their pitch accuracy? How is the sense of time?

SUBJECTIVE ANALYSIS

Only after you have listened to a recording so many times that you know it inside and out are you able to make informed subjective comments. Here is your first opportunity to offer your opinion! Did you like the selection? How did it make you feel? Why did you select this music? Has this listening experience made you curious about another recording, style, artist or group? What aspects made this recording special or unique? Perhaps most important: What have you learned from this recording that you can use to improve your own group?

CHAPTER 12

The Gold Company Program at Western Michigan University

In response to the numerous questions I receive on every aspect of the Vocal Jazz Program at Western Michigan University, I would like to illustrate a typical year in our curriculum. Gold Company is a collegiate vocal jazz program, which is a vital part of an established jazz studies program. **WMU** has an internationally recognized School of Music, where degree offerings include bachelors and masters degrees in jazz studies. After over twenty years of directing this program I have developed a justification and educational philosophy for every facet of the curriculum. These philosophies and justifications evolved from my teaching, conducting and performing experiences, and the successes achieved by students after leaving our university. There is a reason for everything the ensemble does each academic year. If my students ever question any aspect of our curriculum, I encourage them to ask me why we are doing what we are doing!

When I began my tenure at Western Michigan University and was assigned to direct the "pop" vocal ensemble (formerly known as *The Varsity Vagabonds)* that became Gold Company, I knew that I wanted to learn about and teach the most challenging choral literature in the popular idiom. I also knew that it would a tremendous musical challenge for my students and for me. I could continue to grow as a musician and my students would get a great choral education. A definite win/win!

Gold Company originally consisted of 24 singers. After six years, so many students were interested in joining the ensemble that a second vocal jazz ensemble (**GC II**) was added to the curriculum. At the advent of **GC II**, I decided to reduce the number of singers in Gold Company to 16. **GC II** enrollment usually includes between 18-28 singers, and an independent rhythm section and audio crew, depending on the number and quality of students auditioning. Both ensembles sing on a highly artistic level. The primary difference between Gold Company and **GC II** is that the members of **GC II** are usually either less experienced than Gold Company members, or they have less time to commit to the ensemble. The talent and potential of the individuals in **GC II** always amazes me, and it is common for a person to sing for a year or two in **GC II**, then successfully audition for and participate in Gold Company.

AUDITIONS

Auditions for both Gold Company and **GC II** are open to any Western Michigan University student and are held at the start of the academic year. The audition is the same for both ensembles and consists of the following elements:

1 • *Two vocal selections of the student's choice.* Generally I prefer selections in the jazz or pop style, but I am primarily interested in the quality of the voice, so I encourage the student to prepare whatever shows them at their best.

2 • *Sight-reading.* This is an important part of the audition. Because we learn so much repertoire it is vital that the prospective Gold Company member be a

Even if a student has the best voice on the planet, if they can't read music, they will not be in Gold Company.

good sight-reader. Even if a student has the best voice on the planet, if they can't read music, they will not be in Gold Company.

3 • *Aural comprehension.* The student is asked to sing a short melodic phrase played on the piano. This exercise allows me to evaluate the student's ear.

4 • *24-hour piece.* The student receives an excerpt of a choral piece (usually 16-32 measures in length) that I have selected. Generally, this is a challenging vocal jazz piece. All women must learn the alto part, and men have their choice of the tenor or bass part. The next day, the student returns and sings their choral part as a solo, a cappella. The result of the 24-hour piece reveals very much about the attitude, motivation and work ethic of the student. If the student does poorly on their sight-reading exam but gives a great performance on the 24-hour piece, it confirms that the student is capable of learning and retaining challenging music very quickly.

5 • *Audition form and statement of policy.* Each student must complete a three-page audition form and statement of policy. How they actually fill out the form and how well they express themselves in writing has proven to be just as important as their answers to the questions. A sample audition form and statement of policy follows.

6 • *Scat singing.* Each student is asked to improvise vocally. Some students incorporate scat in their prepared pieces. Others sing on 12-bar blues. Even if a person is an inexperienced improviser and this is their first scat experience, we still observe their talent, potential and willingness to try something new.

7 • *Choreography.* There is no dancing or choreography in our audition.

Gold Company Program
Audition and Interview Form

Name _____

AUDITION PIECES

1 _____

2 _____

School Address _____

School Phone _____

Social Security number _____

Parent's name(s) _____

Parent's address(es) _____

Home phone _____

Questionaire

1. Are you currently enrolled at Western Michigan University? ❑ Yes ❑ No

2. Total number of credits for which you are registered semester _____

3. Are you on probation of any kind? ❑ Yes ❑ No

   (Please specify)_____

4. Your major _____

5. Class year _____

6. Grade point average _____

7. High school attended _____

8. High school music director(s) _____

9. Home town newspaper (full name and town) _____

10. Previous choral experience_____

11. Previous jazz experience _____

12. Previous show choir experience_____

13. Which instruments do you play, how well, and how long? _____

    _____

14. List voice and instrument teachers and length of time with each _____

    _____

    _____

15. List any prescription medications you now take, indicating condition for which you are being
    treated _____

    _____

16. Do you have perfect pitch? ❑ Yes ❑ No

17. Do you transcribe jazz music? ❑ Yes ❑ No

18. Do you compose or arrange jazz/popular music? ❑ Yes ❑ No

19. Are you interested in a leadership position in either group? ❑ Yes ❑ No

Explain _____

_____

20. List dance experience _____

21. List choreography experience _____

22. List theatre experience _____

23. List other music ensembles for which you are auditioning or plan to participate in

_____

_____

24. List any additional special talents, abilities and/or interests, such as impersonations, juggling, story telling, creative writing, art, etc. _____

_____

25. Will you be on campus all year? ❑ Yes ❑ No

26. Are you willing to participate in extra rehearsals as needed? ❑ Yes ❑ No

A&i • page 4

27. Exactly why are you auditioning for one of these groups? _____

_____

28. Describe your music theory background and skill level _____

_____

_____

29. Anything further you would care to add? _____

_____

_____

_____

30. Will you accept a position in either ensemble? ❏ Yes ❏ No

31. If not, which ensemble are you interested in? ❏ GC ❏ GC II

Physical Data

Height _____ Weight _____ T-shirt size _____

Sweatshirt size _____ Female dress size _____ Male jacket size _____

Male waist size _____ Male inseam _____

I usually sing

❏ Soprano ❏ Alto ❏ Tenor ❏ Bass

Your highest note _____ Your lowest note _____

Gold Company
Statement of Policy

The GOLD COMPANY PROGRAM, which includes Gold Company and GC II, enlists students who put the ensemble ahead of self, who are dependable, respectful of others, emotionally mature, wise in the scheduling of their time, and committed to the pursuit of musical and academic excellence.

The GOLD COMPANY PROGRAM can be demanding of a student's time and energy. The total amount of rehearsal and performance time will exceed the catalog listing of class meeting times.

You will be expected to:

- attend all rehearsals with a positive attitude

- be available for all sectionals scheduled by the section leaders

- devote as much individual practice time as needed for preparing your parts outside of rehearsal time

- maintain high standards in your chosen academic pursuits

Although the GOLD COMPANY PROGRAM performance schedule cannot be published in full at the beginning of the year, as a member of either group you commit yourself to the schedule of rehearsals and performances included within this document. All unscheduled appearances will be discussed and voted on by the group involved. A majority YES vote will require that all members of that group participate in that performance.

There are financial responsibilities that Gold Company members will incur. Each member of the GOLD COMPANY PROGRAM must purchase the selected group outfit, pay a percentage of the fall weekend retreat fee ($50), and possibly pay partial expenses for extended tours.

All members of Gold Company are required to:

- accept membership for the entire academic year

- accept a place in a group, if offered, depending on audition results

- indicate by your signature below that you willingly accept all points in this Gold Company statement of policy

Signature _____

Once we have posted audition results we charge into rehearsals with excitement, enthusiasm and passion! Gold Company rehearses approximately five hours per week, with additional sectional rehearsals. The students enroll for one credit per semester and commit to two semesters (the entire academic year). No student is guaranteed a place in the ensemble. All returning students must re-audition and compete with everyone. In any given year there will be some turnover in the personnel of the ensemble, usually about 50%. As a result, there is a base of experience along with the infusion of new blood. We begin with several pieces that are staples of our repertoire. These pieces are either excellent for vocal jazz pedagogy, or are pieces that we have recorded that audiences expect (and like) to hear. Additionally, having a basic repertoire requires the new members to immediately achieve a high level of musicianship, with the benefit of veteran Gold Company members as a sonic model for musical and stylistic guidance.

After two to three weeks of rehearsals, we take a weekend retreat where Gold Company rehearses music and some choreography, and also performs pre-assigned musical projects that include solo songs, improvisation, skits, and a cappella duets. I have found that the ensemble makes three to four weeks of progress during the weekend retreat. As a by-product of the retreat, we are also able to establish an intense work ethic, and the group tends to become closer personally.

We generally accept invitations to give performances after approximately 5 weeks of rehearsal. After that time we are able to perform approximately 45 minutes of memorized music in a program that includes vocal jazz, choreography, specialty acts, and band features. This way, our repertoire and presentation appeals to a wide variety of public and private audiences, ranging from high school students to retirement parties. Our annual on-campus fall concert is called "Sneak Preview" and features the public debut of Gold Company and **GC II**. Each group offers their own set of music and sometimes the groups combine forces on a piece or two. There is no competition between Gold Company and **GC II**, and in fact we encourage a family philosophy where we are all part of a wonderful program.

MILLER SHOW

We are fortunate to have the James W. Miller Auditorium, a 3,500 seat, professionally staffed concert hall on the campus of Western Michigan University. This auditorium is a venue for many major national and international touring companies and artists.

In the winter semester Gold Company presents our main home concert in Miller Auditorium. We combine the members of Gold Company and **GC II**, and present this concert twice in the same day (2 and 8 PM usually on the second Saturday in February) with over 5,000 people in attendance. The audience includes young children, high school and university students, parents, grandparents and everyone in between! This means that there are a wide variety of musical tastes to appeal to, and one of our challenges is to include something for everyone in the audience. This production is our only performance during the year when we combine vocal jazz with extensive choreography, production numbers, specialty acts, elaborate custom-designed sets, lights, numerous costume changes, and comedy! The large production numbers are directed, written, choreographed, arranged and performed by the students in the vocal jazz program. The general public loves this unique and original production, the students have an opportunity to produce and promote an event that is presented at a professional level - and the music and musicianship are never sacrificed. The result is yet another win/win situation. Our students have a tremendous performance opportunity and a wonderful educational experience, and we develop a larger audience for vocal jazz, as many people in the audience are exposed to the vocal jazz idiom for the first time. Our philosophy for this concert is that through diversity of music, programming, choreography and style, everyone in the audience may not like *everything* in the program, but everyone will enjoy *something* in the program.

In a Gold Company performance, very little is unrehearsed or left to chance. In addition to rehearsal time spent on the vocal and instrumental music, we also practice performing and singing with our "look." We do not subscribe to the concept of saving energy for the performance. We rehearse stage entrances, transitions between pieces, position shifts, where we focus our look, how to stand on stage, bows and exits. We incorporate all of these extra-musical considerations into our rehearsals well in advance of our first performance, so that these aspects of the performance appear to be effortless and natural for each individual performer. These suggestions do not represent a large commitment of rehearsal time, but the return on your investment in terms of the professional appearance of your ensemble is well worth it.

Our philosophy for this concert is that through diversity of music, programming, choreography and style, everyone in the audience may not like everything in the program, but everyone will enjoy something in the program.

VOCAL JAZZ FESTIVAL

In the spring we host a vocal jazz festival which typically attracts 25 high school and college vocal jazz ensembles from throughout the United States and Canada. Our festival could easily be twice as large, but we choose to limit participation. The festival is non-competitive, friendly, supportive and educational in nature; every group supports the other performers. Everyone has a great time and everyone comes away from the festival a winner! We love hearing other groups perform and always are a supportive and sympathetic audience. Each participating group receives written and recorded comments, as well as a clinic with an adjudicator immediately following their performance. The evening concert features Gold Company. On the night before the festival we feature a guest artist or group. In the past we have hosted Bobby McFerrin, New York Voices, The Real Group, Jon Hendricks, The Hi-Lo's, Janis Siegel, Mark Murphy, Bonnie Herman, Take 6, Sunny Wilkinson, and Kurt Elling, among many others.

RECORDING STUDIO

We are fortunate to have a 48-track state of the art recording studio within the School of Music at Western Michigan University. I believe it is an important part of our curriculum to give our students recording studio experience. We are also fortunate to have the opportunity to record demo CD's for several major music publishing companies. These recordings are heard by choral directors throughout the world, therefore, we challenge our students to produce a product that matches the quality of professional recordings. In addition to our demo recordings, we record and produce Gold Company CD's. Our CD's highlight the talents of our student musicians, arrangers, composers and studio technicians. Again, due to the high visibility of our program, we challenge ourselves to create a musical and technical product that will serve to educate, entertain and inspire the listener.

THE GOLD COMPANY BAND

Auditions for our instrumental ensembles also occur at the beginning of the academic year. We hold auditions/interviews for piano, bass, drums, guitar, trumpet, tenor saxophone, and trombone. Usually we are able to attract talented and accomplished instrumentalists because the players with the highest HQ's realize that participation in Gold Company will provide them with extraordinary opportunities including:

- making music on a very high level

- playing in a wide variety of styles

- working on studio recordings

- participating in remarkable performance experiences

Once the band is chosen, I give them charts and send them away to learn the material on their own. There is no need to bring them into the vocal rehearsal at this point because the singers need to develop as an a cappella ensemble before we add instrumental accompaniment. Once the band has learned the Gold Company repertoire, I require them to learn separate instrumental material that can also be programmed into performances. The singers and the instrumentalists are required to memorize their music. We will typically add the band to rehearsals after three weeks of a cappella singing. Subsequently the band will usually come to rehearsal only one or two hours per week (as a courtesy to the players, and in the interest of rehearsal efficiency), as the vocals continue to be emphasized. The band is a vital and integral part of our programs, and there is mutual respect between the singers and instrumentalists.

TECHNICAL CREW

At the beginning of the academic year when we hold Gold Company vocal and instrumental auditions, we also interview students interested in participating as audio technicians. Prior experience and knowledge of sound systems is not a prerequisite for the job, but a great attitude and a willingness to learn are. We select two to four students and assign them to each ensemble. Their duties include the supervision, care and repair of our audio equipment. They also supervise the assembly and removal of the sound system at rehearsals and performances. Finally, they have the most important responsibility of mixing the ensemble sound in performance. Ultimately, the sound that reaches our audience rests in their hands. It is crucial that you teach and train the audio crew to listen to the ensemble with director ears and to know the appropriate sound, balance and dynamic for each piece of music in the show.

It is crucial that you teach and train the audio crew to listen to the ensemble with director ears and to know the appropriate sound, balance and dynamic for each piece of music in the show.

In Gold Company we assign specific **PA** system set-up duties and tasks to each and every member of the ensemble: male and female singers, instrumentalists, and crew. This requirement serves three purposes. First, it familiarizes our students with the sound system, thereby giving them valuable knowledge of its function. Through repetition and habit, we are able to achieve efficiency and consistency in our set-up procedure as well as the appearance of our stage set (including the specific placement of risers, instruments and each component of the **PA** system). Secondly, through cooperation, teamwork and practice we are able to become a well-oiled machine and establish a fast and consistent routine in our set-ups. This results in more time that can be used for rehearsals, sound checks, dressing room time, and, perhaps most important to my students, the consumption of food! Last, and perhaps most important, having everyone involved in the assembly and removal of the sound system leaves little opportunity for performers to develop an attitude of superiority or condescension toward the members of the tech crew. That kind of thinking will ultimately have a negative effect on any ensemble.

TRAVEL

Each year the ensemble takes an extended tour, usually during the first week of summer vacation. By this time, the ensemble is doing its best singing and the students do not have the pressure of academic assignments. Gold Company has performed throughout the United States, Canada and Europe. We generally travel with our own sound system. If that is impossible, then we must be assured that we will be provided with a specific **PA** system that meets all of our technical requirements. Tours can create wonderful experiences and fond memories, but they are also quite grueling. Many students who have indicated that they would like to have a professional life "on the road" change their minds when greeted with the harsh realities and difficulties of that life. Suffice it to say, a tour gives the student an educational opportunity that cannot be found in the classroom.

PROJECTS

In addition to rehearsals and ensemble singing, we regularly require independent projects of our students that raise their **HQ**'s and improve their musical skill and sophistication. These include:

1 • *Listening assignment.* Students write a detailed report on an appropriate musical selection of their choice.

2 • *Scat assignment.* A recorded improvised solo is transcribed and sung along with the original artist.

3 • *Keyboard assignment.* A ii-V7-I progression is performed in all 12 keys.

4 • *Vocal/Keyboard assignment.* Students accompany themselves at the piano on an appropriate song of their choice.

We have very high expectations of our students. We encourage a mature attitude, independence and individual responsibility. An alumnus of our program should be a smart musician, not a dumb singer. Their knowledge of vocal groups and soloists, styles, history and jazz theory should be extensive, and their love for the art of vocal jazz should be something that they carry with them throughout their lives.

GOLD COMPANY PA SYSTEM SPECIFICATIONS

SOUND BOARD

Yamaha M-2000 32 Channel

AMPLIFIERS

3 QSC Power Light (1800 watts)
1 QSC Power Light (3400 watts)

MICROPHONES

Vocals	16 Shure Beta 58	
Vocal solos	4 Shure Beta 87	
	4 Shure Beta 87 U/C Series UHF wireless	
Horns	7 Shure Beta 56	
Snare drum and guitar	6 Shure Beta 57	
Overhead on drums and high hat.	4 Shure SM-81	
Bass Drum	1 AKG D-112	
Piano	1 Barcus-Berry Piano pick-up	

SPEAKERS

    4 ElectroVoice XI-115 Mid High Speaker Cabinets

    2 ElectroVoice Dual 18-inch Sub Cabinets

    8 ElectroVoice 12 x 1 monitor wedges

    1 Ashley two-channel, three-way crossover

PROCESSING EQUIPMENT

    1 Behringer Ultra-Curve Pro (Digital **EQ**) 24-bit Dual – DPS Main Frame model (DPS 8024)

    3 Ashley GQX Dual 31 Band **EQ**'s (Analog **EQ**) Model 3102

    1 Lexicon PCM 81 (Digital Effects)

    1 TC Electronics m-2000 (Digital effects)

    2 DBX 166A Compressor/Limiter

    1 DBX 166XL Compressor/Limiter

PLAYBACK/RECORDING

    1 Tascam CD/Cassette Combo player (CD-A500)

    1 Tascam DAT Recorder/Player (DA 30 MKII)

    1 Tascam DA 88 8 track digital recorder

MICROPHONE CABLES AND SNAKE

Pro-Co

MIC STANDS AND T-BARS

Atlas TM1 (T-BAR)

Assortment of straight stands and "boom" stands (all the same color and style)

Glossary

A

A CAPPELLA
Music sung without instrumental accompaniment.

AABA
A standard 32-measure song form consisting of four separate phrases eight measures long. *I Got Rhythm* by George Gershwin is a well-known example (not to be confused with the pop vocal group).

AMP
Abbreviation for amplifier. Component in the **PA** system that provides the power to make instruments and voices louder.

AXE (OR AX)
Used to describe a musical instrument, such as a trumpet or saxophone.

B

BACK BEAT
Accents on beats two and four in swing and rock, usually played by the drummer.

BALLAD
A piece of music in a slow tempo; usually refers to a standard tune.

BLOWING
Improvising, as in "blowing over the changes."

BOP
Or bebop. A style of jazz that developed in the 1940's that uses intricate eighth note based melodies with quick harmonic rhythm.

BOSSA NOVA
An even eighth note style of music with origins in Brazil.

BRIDGE
The **B** section of an **AABA** tune (also known as the *release* or the *channel*)

C

CABLE
The cord that connects microphones or speakers to an amplifier.

CHANGES
The chord progression of a piece of music, as in "Use the blues changes."

CHART
A written out musical score; usually refers to a particular arrangement.

CHOPS

Used to describe a person's musical abilities (vocal or instrumental), as in "She has terrific chops."

CHORUS

A section of a song. The chorus usually follows the verse of a song.

CLAVE(S)

Refers to either a specific (Cuban-derived) dance rhythm or a percussion instrument (see Chapter 3, page 8).

COMBO

A small group (three to ten) of musicians.

COMP

Short for improvised accompaniment, as in "Comp behind the soloist." Usually reserved for pianists and guitarists.

D

DOUBLE TIME

Literally "double the tempo." Play or sing twice as fast. Also common is "double time feel" which means that the rhythm section should imply that an eighth note equals a quarter note, but the underlying tempo stays the same.

E

EQ

Abbreviation for equalizer or equalization. Refers to the balance of high and low frequencies running through a sound board.

F

FALL (OR FALL OFF)

An effect in which the pitch of a note drops an unspecified duration and interval.

FAKE BOOK

A collection of songs that include only the melody and chord changes (and possibly lyrics) for each piece. In performance, jazz musicians improvise or fake the tune based on this information. See *lead sheet*.

FUSION

A style of music that combines elements of gospel, blues, rock and/or jazz.

FILL

A short, improvised segment (played by a harmonic instrument and/or the drums) that helps connect phrases or sections in a piece of music.

FREE JAZZ

Music that is completely improvised. There is no set form, harmony or rhythmic pulse (not to be confused with "No Cover Charge").

G

GIG

A performance, as in "The gig starts at eight o'clock."

GLISSANDO

Playing or singing all the notes between two set pitches; sometimes referred as a smear.

GROOVE

The rhythmic feel of a particular composition or section of a composition.

H

HALF TIME

Literally, play or sing half as fast; the opposite of double time.

HEAD

The original melody of the piece being performed, as in "Play the head twice before the solo section." May also refer to the "top" or beginning of a chart.

I

IN THE POCKET

Used by jazz musicians to describe the perfect rhythmic feel of a composition, as in "The Basie band had that one in the pocket."

INTRO

The beginning of a piece, usually not played again during the statement of the melody or during improvised solos. Typically four or eight bars long.

J

JAM SESSION

A gathering of jazz musicians to play music. "Jam" implies that there are no written arrangements, but that the players use standard tunes they have memorized to perform as the basis for improvisation.

L

LATIN

A generic term used to describe many types of music based on even eighth note patterns rather than the uneven eights of *swing* (see Chapter 3, page 8).

LEAD SHEET

Written music that may include the melody, chords and/or lyrics of a song (see Appendix III, page 108). A fake book is a collection of lead sheets.

LICK

A short melodic segment in a piece of music or improvised solo.

M

MIXER

The component in a sound system used to blend and balance signals being received from microphones. See *soundboard*.

MONITOR

A speaker used on stage to enable the musicians to hear themselves sing or play.

MONTUNO

A recurring melodic and rhythmic phrase in some types of latin music (see Chapter 3, page 8).

P

PA SYSTEM

Public address system. A somewhat antiquated term synonymous with *sound system* or *sound reinforcement system*.

R

RIDE CYMBAL

One of the cymbals used by a drum set player to create a swing feel (see Chapter 6, page 34).

RIFF

A short, repeated melodic segment.

RHYTHM CHANGES

The set of chord changes specific to the Gershwin song *I Got Rhythm*.

RHYTHM SECTION

Specific part or group of a performing ensemble that typically includes guitar, piano, bass, drum set and/or percussion.

S

SALSA

A specific style of latin jazz originating in Cuba and Puerto Rico (see Chapter 3, page 8).

SAMBA

A dance form with roots in Brazil. The samba is usually faster than a bossa nova and is often coupled with the partito alto (see Chapter 3, page 8).

SCAT SINGING

Vocal improvisation using nonsense syllables such as *doo, dah, diddly*, etc.

SHAKE

An effect used in vocal and instrumental jazz. The shake is similar to a trill but usually rises up to a minor third above the principal pitch.

SIGNAL FLOW

Used to describe the movement of energy (sound) through a sound reinforcement system.

SNAKE

Multiple microphone cables bundled together to provide an efficient extension cord from the stage mics to the sound board.

SNARE

The part of a drum set usually used to provide accents, fills and back beat on beats two and four. Snare may also refer to the actual mechanism on the bottom head of the drum (see Chapter 6, page 34).

SOUNDBOARD

The component in a sound system used to blend and balance signals being received from microphones. See *mixer*.

STANDARD

A piece of music from the body of repertoire composed by great American songwriters including George Gershwin, Cole Porter, Harold Arlen, Duke Ellington, Jerome Kern, Irving Berlin, Richard Rodgers, and others.

STOP TIME

A section in a composition where there is punctuation only on certain beats. For example, a blues tune might have a stop time section where the rhythm section only plays on beat one of each measure, while the soloist improvises.

SWING

Refers to the style of music made popular by the dance bands of the 1940s, as in "*In The Mood* is a swing chart." Also refers to the rhythmic placement of eighth notes common in jazz (see chapter 3, page 8).

SYNCOPATION

Emphasis on a beat or a part of the beat that is not expected or normally emphasized.

T

TAG

Extra measures added at the end of a piece to conclude the composition.

TURNAROUND

Typically the last two measures of a song or of an eight bar phrase that propel the harmony to the next key center using the chord progression I-vi-ii-V or iii-vi-ii-V . For example, in the key of C, Emi7 to Ami7 to Dmi7 to G7 would be a common turnaround.

TWELVE BAR BLUES

A song form that implies a specific form and harmony (see Chapter 5, page 26).

V

VAMP

A short chord progression (typically two or four measures in length) that is repeated ad lib. Usually used in introductions and tags.

VERTICAL STRUCTURE

A chord, or set of "stacked pitches."

VOCALESE

Singing original lyrics set to the notes of a previously-recorded instrumental jazz improvisation. Great practitioners included Eddie Jefferson and Jon Hendricks.

VOICING

The structural arrangement of notes used by pianists, guitarists, composers and arrangers.

W

WALKING BASS LINE

An improvised or written bass part comprised mainly of primary beats outlining the harmony.

Appendix I: Vocal Jazz Discography

Updates to this discography can be found online at www.lorenz.com.

The following should be considered essential recordings when building a vocal jazz collection from scratch. (Do Not Pass Go, Do Not Collect $200...)

ANTHOLOGIES/COLLECTIONS OF ARTISTS

ARTIST	LABEL & NO.
Anthology of Scat Singing, Vol. 1	Masters of Jazz 801
Anthology of Scat Singing, Vol. 2	Masters of Jazz 802
Anthology of Scat Singing, Vol. 3	Masters of Jazz 803
The Jazz Singers: A Smithsonian Collection of Jazz Vocals from 1919 to 1994	Smithsonian 0040
Terence Blanchard: Let's Get Lost	Sony Classical 89607
Ray Brown: Some of My Best Friends Are Singers	Telarc 83441

VOCAL GROUPS

ARTIST	TITLE
Chanticleer	Lost in the Stars
	Free Fall
Four Freshmen	All-Time Favorites
The Hi-Lo's	Best of the Columbia Years
The King's Singers	Get Happy
Lambert, Hendricks & Ross	Greatest Hits
Manhattan Transfer	Best of Manhattan Transfer
	Vocalese
New York Voices	Sing, Sing, Sing
The Real Group	Unreal!
The Singers Unlimited	Magic Voices
Swingle Singers	Jazz Sebastian Bach
Take 6	Greatest Hits

FEMALE VOCALISTS

ARTIST	TITLE
Ernestine Anderson	A Perfect Match
Dee Dee Bridgewater	Love and Peace: A Tribute to Horace Silver
Betty Carter	The Audience with Betty Carter
Ella Fitzgerald	Montreux '77: Ella Fitzgerald with Tommy Flanagan
	Sings the George and Ira Gershwin Songbook
Billie Holiday	The Complete Billie Holiday On Verve 1945-59
Shirley Horn	Here's to Life
Nancy King	Straight Into Your Heart
Diana Krall	When I Look in Your Eyes
Cleo Laine	Live at Carnegie Hall
Abbey Lincoln	You Gotta Pay the Band
Carmen McRae	The Best of Carmen McRae
Dianne Reeves	The Calling
Elis Regina	Elis e Tom
Sarah Vaughan	Sarah Vaughan Live in Japan, Vol. 1
	Sarah Vaughan Live in Japan, Vol. 2
Sunny Wilkinson	High Wire
Cassandra Wilson	Traveling Miles
Nancy Wilson	Nancy Wilson/Cannonball Adderly

MALE VOCALISTS

ARTIST	TITLE
Louis Armstrong	Jazz Masters 24: Ella Fitzgerald-Louis Armstrong
Chet Baker	Let's Get Lost: The Best of Chet Baker Sings
Tony Bennett	Perfectly Frank
	The Tony Bennett/Bill Evans Album
Nat "King" Cole	Love Is Here to Stay
Harry Connick, Jr.	When Harry Met Sally

The recordings listed here should by no means be considered the definite list. This list is not meant to be comprehensive; rather, it should serve as representative of the total output of selected vocal groups and solo singers. The list was current at the time of publication, but I encourage you to seek new releases, as well as many of the recordings unintentionally not mentioned here.

MALE VOCALISTS (CONTINUED)

ARTIST	TITLE
Kurt Elling	*Live in Chicago*
João Gilberto	*Amoroso/Brasil*
Johnny Hartman	*John Coltrane & Johnny Hartman*
Jon Hendricks	*Freddie Freeloader*
Al Jarreau	*Live in London*
Eddie Jefferson	*The Jazz Singer*
Kevin Mahogany	*Songs and Moments*
Bobby McFerrin	*Play*
	The Voice
Mark Murphy	*Bop for Kerouac*
	The Nat King Cole Songbook
John Pizzarelli	*New Standards*
Frank Sinatra	*Sinatra at the Sands*
	Sinatra's Swingin' Session
Mel Tormé	*At The Red Mill/Live at the Maisonette*
	Rob McConnell and the Boss Brass
Joe Williams	*Count Basie Swings – Joe Williams Sings*
	Here's to Life

—— EXPANDED DISCOGRAPHY ——

VOCAL GROUPS

ARTIST	TITLE	LABEL & NO.
Beachfront Property	*A Beachfront Christmas*	Cexton 2262
	Beachfront Property	Cexton 1848
	Straight Up	Cexton 0316
Boca Livre	*Dancando Pelas Sombras*	Xeno 4021
The Boswell Sisters	*It's the Girls*	ASV 5014
	Okay, America: Alternate Takes and Rarities	Jass 622
	That's How Rhythm Is Born	Legacy 66997
Chanticleer	*Lost in the Stars*	Teldec 13132
	Out of This World	Teldec 96515
Clare Fischer	*Free Fall*	Discovery 921
	Salsa Picante (2 + 2)	Discovery 817
	Rockin' in Rhythm	JVC 7502
Les Double Six	*Les Double Six*	RCA Victor 65659
First Call	*Beyond December*	Warner Alliance 45947
	Sacred Journey	Word 57291
Four Freshmen	*5 Trombones/5 Trumpets*	Collector's Choice 17
	All-Time Favorites	EMI/Capitol 9170
	Day By Day	Hindsight 604
	Four Freshmen	Capitol 93197
	Fresh!	Ranwood 8241
	Graduation Day	Laserlight 12120
	Greatest Hits	Curb 77612
	In Concert	Hindsight 614
	It's a Blue World	Viper's Nest 170
	Live at Butler University	Creative World 1059
	Spotlight on the Four Freshmen	EMI/Capitol 31205
	Still Fresh	Gold Label 8005
Glad	*A Capella Gershwin*	A&M 161 166
	Color Outside the Lines	CGI 1126
	Glad: The A Capella Collection	Liberty 34187
	Who Do You Love?	Green Tree 2353
The Hi-Lo's	*And All That Jazz*	Collectors Series 75203
	Best of the Columbia Years	Koch Jazz 7926
	Cherries and Other Delights	Hindsight 603
	Clap Yo' Hands	DRG 5184
	Harmony in Jazz	Encore 1438
	Love Nest	Collectors Series 75022

VOCAL GROUPS (CONTINUED)

ARTIST	TITLE	LABEL & NO.
	Now Hear This/Broadway Playbill...	Collectables 6465
	Suddenly It's the Hi-Los/	
	Harmony in Jazz.............	Collectables 6026
	The Best of the Hi-Los: Nice Work	
	if You Can Get It	Varese Vintage 5694
	Together Wherever We Go	Sony 24197
Jackie & Roy	*Concerts By The Sea*.................	Koch Jazz 8546
	Sondheim......................	Red Baron 57338
	The Beautiful Sea.....................	DRG 8574
Just 4 Kicks	*All In Good Time*	Primarily A Capella 6255
	Just For Kicks......................	MNOP 1003
The King Sisters........................	*Spotlight on the King Sisters*	Capitol 31203
The King's Singers......................	*America*.......................	EMI/Angel 49701
	Chanson D'amour	BMG/RCA Victor 61427
	Get Happy!	EMI Classics 54190
The L.A. Jazz Choir	*Sweet Dreams – With the*	
	Mark Davidson Trio	Stage 3 6234
	The L.A. Jazz Choir	Stage 3 10006
	*Rosemany Clooney: Sings Rodgers,	
	Hart and Hammerstein	Concord Jazz 4405
Ladysmith Black Mambazo	*Shaka Zulu*	Warner Bros. 25582
	The Warner Bros. Collection ...	Warner Archives 79986
Lambert, Hendricks & Bavan..............	*Live at Newport '63*	RCA Victor 68731
	Swingin' Till the Girls Come Home	Bluebird 6282
Lambert, Hendricks & Ross	*Everybody's Boppin'*..................	Legacy 45020
	Greatest Hits	Columbia 32911
	Hottest New Group in Jazz..........	Columbia 64933
	Lambert, Hendricks & Ross	Sony 28306
	Sing a Song of Basie	Impulse! 11122
	Sing Ellington	Columbia 8310
	The Swingers!	EMI-Manhattan 46849
	Twisted: Best of Lambert,	
	Hendricks & Ross................	Rhino 70328
Johnny Mann Singers	*Great Band, Great Voices*.............	Liberty 14009
Manhattan Transfer	*Anthology: Down in Birdland*	Rhino 71053
	Best of Manhattan Transfer...........	Atlantic 19319
	Bodies and Souls	Atlantic 80104
	Bop Do Wop.......................	Atlantic 81223
	Brasil............................	Atlantic 81803
	Coming Out.......................	Atlantic 18183
	Extensions	Atlantic 19258
	Man-Tora! Live in Tokyo..............	Rhino 72403
	Mecca for Moderns	Atlantic 16036
	Offbeat of Avenues..................	Columbia 47079
	Pastiche	Rhino 71809
	Snowfall – The Christmas Album	Columbia 52968
	Swing...........................	Atlantic 83012
	Tonin'	Atlantic 82661
	The Manhattan Transfer..............	Atlantic 18133
	The Manhattan Transfer Live	Atlantic 50540
	The Manhattan Transfer Meets	
	Tubby the Tuba	Summit 152
	The Spirit of St. Louis.................	Altantic 83394
	The Very Best of the Manhattan Transfer ..	Rhino 71560
	Vocalese	Atlantic 81266
Phil Mattson & P.M. Singers...............	*Night in the City*	Dark Orchid 14018
The Mills Brothers......................	*Four Boys and a Guitar:*	
	The Essential Mills Brothers	Legacy 57713
MPB 4	*Amigo E Pra Essas Coisas*.............	Som Livre 1098
	Vivo Melhores Momentos..................	Cid 00463

VOCAL GROUPS (CONTINUED)

ARTIST	TITLE	LABEL & NO.
New York Voices	Ancient Tower: The Poetry of Ranier Maria Rilke	Earthbeat 42577
	Hearts of Fire	GRP 9653
	New York Voices	GRP 9589
	New York Voices Collection	GRP 9766
	New York Voices Sing the Songs of Paul Simon	RCA Victor 68872
	Sing, Sing, Sing	Concord Jazz 4961
	What's Inside	GRP 9700
Nylons	Best of the Nylons	Open Air 10308
	Happy Together	Open Air 10306
	Rockapella	Windham Hill 1085
	The Nylons	Attic 1125
Rare Silk	American Eyes	Palo Alto 8086
	Black & Blue	TBA 214
	New Weave	Polydor 422 810 028
The Real Group	Commonly Unique	Gazell 1032
	Debut	Real 1
	Live in Stockholm	Passport/Town Crier 522
	Nothing But the Real Group	Caprice 21376
	One for All	Gazell 1024
	Ori:ginal	Gazell 1010
	Röster	Caprice 21405
	The Real Group	Edenroth 001
	Unreal!	Town Crier 519
The Ritz	Almost Blue	Denon 7999
	Flying	Denon 73673
	Movin' Up	Denon 72526
	The Ritz	Denon 1839
Rockapella	Lucky Seven	Rockapella 1996
The Singers Unlimited	A Capella	Verve/MPS 815 671
	Christmas	Verve/MPS 821 859
	Compact Jazz: The Singers Unlimited	Verve/MPS 831 373
	Feeling Free	Verve/MPS 821 858
	Magic Voices	Verve/MPS 539 130
	Masterpieces	Verve/MPS 523 521
	The Singers Unlimited With Rob McConnell & the Boss Brass	Verve/MPS 817 486
SoVoSo	Bridges	Primarily A Capella 2720
	Truth & Other Stories	Primarily A Capella 2710
	World Jazz A Capella	Primarily A Capella 2700
Sweet Honey In The Rock	Twenty-Five	Rykodisc 10541
Swingle Singers	Anyone For Mozart, Bach, Handel, Vivaldi?	Verve 826 948
	Compact Jazz: The Swingle Singers	Verve 830 701
	Jazz Sebastian Bach	Verve 824 703
	New World	Swingle 10
	The Story of Christmas	Primarily A Capella 6250
Take 6	Brothers	Reprise 46235
	Doo Be Doo Wop Bop	Reprise 25781
	Greatest Hits	Reprise 47375
	He Is Christmas	Reprise 26665
	Join the Band	Reprise 45497
	Live	Reprise 47611
	So Cool	Warner Bros. 46795
	So Much 2 Say	Reprise 25892
	Take 6	Reprise 25670
	We Wish You a Merry Christmas	Reprise 47391
Vocal Sampling	Live in Berlin	Ashe 2008
	Una Forma Mas	Sire 61792

Vox One	*Out There*	Accurate 5019
	Vox One	MPS 206
Zap Mama	*A Ma Zone*	Narada 48412
Gold Company (WMU)	*Solid*	WMU/SMR 2000
	While We're Young	WMU/SMR 2001

FEMALE VOCALISTS

ARTIST	TITLE	LABEL & NO.
Karrin Allyson	*Azure-Té*	Concord Jazz 4641
	Ballads – Remembering John Coltrane	Concord Jazz 4950
	From Paris to Rio	Concord Jazz 4865
Ernestine Anderson	*A Perfect Match*	Concord Jazz 4357
	Ballad Essentials	Concord Jazz 4886
	Great Moments With Ernestine Anderson	Concord Jazz 4582
	Live From Concord to London	Concord Jazz 4054
Leny Andrade	*Embraceable You*	Timeless 365
	Maiden Voyage	Chesky 113
Lil Hardin Armstrong	*Chicago: The Living Legends*	Original. Jazz Cl. 1823
	Lil Hardin Armstrong and Her Swing Orchestra 1936-1940	Classics 564
Eden Atwood	*A Night in the Life*	Concord Jazz 4730
Grazyna Auguscik	*Pastels*	GMA 1724
Patti Austin	*That Secret Place*	GRP 4023
Mildred Bailey	*The Rockin' Chair Lady (1931-1950)*	GRP 644
Patricia Barber	*Café Blue*	Premonition 21810
	Nightclub	Blue Note 27290
	Split	Premonition 90742
Carmen Bradford	*Finally Yours*	Evidence 1030
	With Respect	Evidence 22115
Dee Dee Bridgewater	*Dear Ella*	Verve 537 896
	In Montreux	Verve 511 895
	Love and Peace: A Tribute to Horace Silver	Verve 527 470
Deborah Brown	*Live in Tivoli*	Intermusic 058
Jeri Brown	*A Timeless Place*	Justin Time 70
	Unfolding – The Peacocks	Justin Time 45
Jeanie Bryson	*I Love Being Here With You*	Telarc 83336
	Tonight I Need You So	Telarc 83348
LaVerne Butler	*Blues in the City*	MaxJazz 105
Ann Hampton Callaway	*After Ours*	Denon 18042
	To Ella With Love	Touchwood 2006
Betty Carter	*Feed the Fire*	Verve 523 600
	Finally – Betty Carter	Roulette 95333
	I'm Yours, You're Mine	Verve 533 182
	Look What I Got!	Verve 835 661
	The Audience With Betty Carter	Verve 835 684
	The Carmen McRae/Betty Carter Duets	Verve 529 579
Patti Catchcart	**Tuck & Patti: Paradise Found*	Windham Hill 11336
	*Tuck & Patti: Taking the Long Way Home	Windham Hill 11507
June Christy	*The Complete Capitol Studio Recordings of Kenton/Christy*	Mosaic 163
	The Misty Miss Christy	Capitol 79845
Chris Connor	*Chris*	Bethlehem 75988
	Lover Come Back to Me	Evidence 22110
	Maynard Ferguson/Chris Connor: Two of a Kind	Roulette 37201
Jay Clayton	*Beautiful Love*	Sunnyside 1066
	Circle Dancing	Sunnyside 1076

FEMALE VOCALISTS (CONTINUED)

ARTIST	TITLE	LABEL & NO.
Rosemary Clooney	*Dedicated to Nelson*	Concord Jazz 4685
	Demi-Centennial: A Girl Singer's Golden Anniversary	Concord Jazz 4633
	Do You Miss New York?	Concord Jazz 4537
	Girl Singer	Concord Jazz 4496
Natalie Cole	*Stardust*	Elektra 61946
	Unforgettable: With Love, Natalie Cole	Elektra 61049
Carla Cook	*Dem Bones*	Maxjazz 111
	It's all About Love	Maxjazz 106
Gal Costa	*Minha Voz, Minha Vida*	Universal Latino 548 274
Meredith D'Ambrosio	*Beware Of Spring*	Sunnyside 1069
	South to a Warmer Place	Sunnyside 1039
Dee Daniels	*All of Me*	September 5101
	Close Encounters of the Swingin' Kind	Timeless 312
Blossom Dearie	*Blossom Dearie*	Verve 837 934
	Give Him the Ooh-La-La	Verve 517 067
Dena DeRose	*I Can See Clearly Now*	Sharp Nine 1018
Trudy Desmond	*Make Me Rainbows*	Koch Jazz 7803
	R.S.V.P.	Jazz Alliance 1010
Ann Dyer	*Revolver: A New Spin*	Premonition 90745
Dominique Eade	*My Resistance Is Low*	Accurate 3925
	When the Wind Was Cool	RCA Victor 68858
Madeline Eastman	*Art Attack*	Mad-Kat 1005
	Mad About Madeline!	Mad-Kat 1003
Eliane Elias	*Eliane Elias Sings Jobim*	Blue Note 95050
	Everything I Love	Blue Note 20827
	Fantasia	Blue Note 96146
Marty Elkins	*Fuse Blues*	Nagel Heyer 062
Cesaria Evora	*Sao Vicente*	Windham Hill 11590
Rachelle Ferrell	*First Instrument*	Blue Note 27820
Ella Fitzgerald	*75th Birthday Celebration*	Uni/Decca 619
	Ella and Basie	Verve 521 411
	Ella and Oscar	Pablo 759
	Ella in Rome: The Birthday Concert	Verve 823 454
	Fitzgerald and Pass... Again	Pablo 772
	Ken Burns' JAZZ: The Definitive Ella Fitzgerald	Verve 594 087
	Montreux '77: Ella Fitzgerald With Tommy Flanagan	Original Jazz Cl. 376
	Newport Jazz Festival/ Live at Carnegie Hall	Columbia 66809
	Sings the George and Ira Gershwin Songbook	Verve 539 759
	Take Love Easy	Pablo 702
	The Complete Ella in Berlin: Mack the Knife	Verve 519 564

NOTE: In addition to the Gershwin Songbook, Ella recorded several other "songbook" projects for Verve, including Harold Arlen, Irving Berlin, Duke Ellington, Jerome Kern, Johnny Mercer, Cole Porter, and Rodgers and Hart.

Verve has released several boxed sets of Ella Fitzgerald, including *The Complete Ella Fitzgerald & Louis Armstrong on Verve* (537 284) and *The Complete Ella Fitzgerald Song Books* (519 832).

Nnenna Freelon	*Listen*	Columbia 64323
	Maiden Voyage	Concord Jazz 4794
	Soul Call	Concord Jazz 4896
Astrud Gilberto	*Finest Hour*	Verve 520 790
	Gilberto Plus the James Last Orchestra	Verve 831 123
	Jazz Masters 9	Verve 519 824
Bebel Gilberto	*Tanto Tempo*	Six Degrees 1026
Gabrielle Goodman	*Travelin' Light*	JMT 514 006

FEMALE VOCALISTS (CONTINUED)

ARTIST	TITLE	LABEL & NO.
Angela Hagenbach	Weaver of Dreams	Amazon 3344
Michelle Hendricks	Carryin' On	Muse 5336
	Keepin' Me Satisfied	Muse 5363
	Me and My Shadow	Muse 5404
Billie Holiday	As Time Goes By	Drive Archives 41024
	Billie Holiday at Carnegie Hall	Verve 527 777
	Lady In Autumn: The Best of the Verve Years	Verve 849 434
	The Complete Billie Holiday on Verve 1945-59	Verve 513 859
	The Essential Billie Holiday: Songs of Lost Love	PGD/Polygram 517 172
Shirley Horn	Here's to Life	Verve 511 879
	I Remember Miles	Verve 557 119
	The Main Ingredient	Verve 529 555
	You Won't Forget Me	Verve 847 482
	You're My Thrill	Verve 549 417
Lena Horne	Being Myself	Blue Note 34286
	Love Is the Thing	BMG 66473
Miki Howard	Miki Sings Billie: A Tribute to Billie Holiday	Giant 24521
	Three Wishes	Peak 8502
Helen Humes	Swingin' With Helen	Original Jazz Cl. 608
	'Tain't Nobody's Biz-ness if I Do	Original Jazz Cl. 453
Etta Jones	Don't Go to Strangers	Original Jazz Cl. 298
	From the Heart	Original Jazz Cl. 1016
Sheila Jordan	Portrait of Sheila	Blue Note 89002
	Songs From Within	M.A. 014
Joyce	Language and Love	Verve Forecast 849 195
Stacey Kent	Dreamsville*	Candid 79775
Angelique Kidjo	Keep on Moving: The Best Of	Columbia 85758
Nancy King	King of the Road	Orb 5817
	Straight into Your Heart	Mons 874878
Miriam Klein	Ladylike	MPS 523 379
Kristin Korb	Introducing Kristin Korb With The Ray Brown Trio	Telarc 83386
Irene Kral	Better Than Anything	Ava 33
	Kral Space	Collectables 7160
	You Are There	Audiophile 299
Diana Krall	All for You	Impulse! 182
	Love Scenes	Impulse! 233
	The Look of Love	Verve 549 846
	When I Look in Your Eyes	Verve 304
Karin Krog	Jubilee: The Best of 30 Years	Verve 527 316
	Some Other Spring	Storyville 4045
Cleo Laine	Born on a Friday	RCA Victor 5113
	Live at Carnegie Hall	RCA Victor 3751
	Nothing Without You	Concord Jazz 4515
	Solitude	RCA Victor 68124
Mary LaRose	Walking Woman	GM 3041
Peggy Lee	Best of Big Bands: Benny Goodman, Featuring Peggy Lee	Columbia 53422
	Fever and Other Hits	CEMA 57358
	The Best of the Capitol Years	Capitol 21204
Ranee Lee	Deep Song	Justin Time 33
	You Must Believe in Swing	Justin Time 88
Kevyn Lettau	Another Season	JVC 2030
	Kevyn Lettau	Samson 29916
	Universal Language	JVC 2048

FEMALE VOCALISTS (CONTINUED)

ARTIST	TITLE	LABEL & NO.
Abbey Lincoln	Over the Years	Verve 549 101
	Wholly Earth	Verve 559 538
	You Gotta Pay the Band	Verve 511 110
Carmen Lundy	Old Devil Moon	JVC 2065
Nancy Marano	A Perfect Match	Denon 79470
Kitty Margolis	Evolution	Mad-Kat 1004
	Straight Up With a Twist	Mad-Kat 1006
Tania Maria	Bluesilian	TKM 5003
	No Comment	TKM 5001
	Outrageous	Concord Picante 4653
Claire Martin	Make This City Ours	Linn 066
	Off Beat	Linn 049
Laurel Massé	Feather and Bone	Premonition 90571
Susannah McCorkle	From Bessie To Brazil	Concord Jazz 4547
	From Broadway to Bebop	Concord Jazz 4715
Carmen McRae	Ballad Essentials	Concord Jazz 4877
	Carmen Sings Monk	Novus 3086
	Dream of Life	Qwest 43640
	Heat Wave	Concord Jazz 4189
	The Best of Carmen McRae	Blue Note 33578
	The Carmen McRae/Betty Carter Duets	Verve 529 579
	The Great American Songbook	Atlantic 2904
	You're Lookin' at Me	Concord Jazz 4235
Helen Merrill	Brownie: An Homage to Clifford Brown	Verve 522 363
	Jelena Ana Milcetic	Verve 543 089
	You and the Night and the Music	Verve 537 087
Joni Mitchell	Both Sides Now	Reprise 47620
	Mingus	Elektra 505
	Shadows and Light	Elektra 704
Jane Monheit	Come Dream With Me	Warlock 4219
	Never Never Land	N-Coded 64207
Marisa Monte	A Great Noise	Blue Note 53353
	Memories, Chronicles and Declarations of Love	Blue Note 27085
Shawnn Monteiro	Visit Me	Monad 95
Stephanie Nakasian	Bitter Sweet	Jazz Mania 6002
	Invitation to an Escapade	Chase 8060
Judy Neimack	Heart's Desire	Stash 548
	Mingus, Monk & Mal	Freelance 021
Caecilie Norby	Caecilie Norby	Blue Note 32202
Anita O'Day	Anita O'Day's Finest Hour	Verve 543 600
	Rust of the Road	Pablo 950
	Swings Cole Porter With Billy May	Verve 849 266
Rebecca Parris	A Beautiful Friendship	Allenburgh 0019
	My Foolish Heart	Koch Jazz 7887
Zizi Possi	Puro Prazer	Musicrama 0
Rosa Passos	The Best of Rosa Passos	Velas 1004
Flora Purim	Perpetual Emotion	Narada 50625
	Queen of the Night	Sound Wave 89009
	Wings of Imaginations	Concord Vista 4973
Judy Rafat	Con Alma: A Tribute to Dizzy Gillspie	Timeless 448
Ma Rainey	Ma Rainey	Milestone 47021
Dianne Reeves	Dianne Reeves	Blue Note 46906
	I Remember	Blue Note 90264
	In the Moment: Live in Concert	Blue Note 25141
	The Calling	Blue Note 27694
Elis Regina	Elis E Tom	Philips 824 418
	Mestre Sala Dos Mares	EPM 197302
	Montreux Jazz Festival	WEA 54933
	Personalidade (Best of Brazil)	Verve 514 135

FEMALE VOCALISTS (CONTINUED)

ARTIST	TITLE	LABEL & NO.
Betty Roche	Lightly and Politely	Original Jazz Cl. 1802
	Singin' & Swingin'	Original Jazz Cl. 1718
Virginia Rodrigues	Nós	Hannibal 1448
Annie Ross	Music Is Forever	DRG 91446
	Skylark	DRG 8470
Vanessa Rubin	I'm Glad There Is You: A Tribute to Carmen McRae	Novus 63170
Diane Schuur	Deedles	GRP 9510
	Dianne Schuur & The Count Basie Orchestra	GRP 9550
	Timeless	GRP 9540
Cathy Segal-Garcia	Heart to Heart	HD 501
	Song of the Heart	Sunshine 1001
Kendra Shank	Reflections	Jazz Focus 37
Janis Siegel	Slow Hot Wind	Varese 5552
	The Tender Trap	Monarch 1021
Judi Silvano	Songs I Wrote or Wish I Did	JSL 0003
	Vocalise	Blue Note 52390
Nina Simone	Jazz Masters 17	Verve 518 198
	Little Girl Blue	Bethlehem 30042
Carol Sloane	Ballad Essentials	Concord Jazz 4971
	Romantic Ellington	DRG 8480
	The Real Thing	Contemporary 14060
	The Songs Ella & Louis Sang	Concord Jazz 1260
Bessie Smith	The Complete Recordings, Vol. 1	Sony 47091
	The Complete Recordings, Vol. 2	Sony 47471
Keely Smith	Keely Sings Sinatra	Concord Jazz 4943
	Swing, Swing, Swing	Concord Jazz 4842
Jeri Southern	Jeri Southern Meets Cole Porter/ At The Crescendo	EMI 112
	The Very Thought of You: The Decca Years 1951-57	GRP 671
Jo Stafford	Haunted Heart	Verve 078
	Spotlight on Jo Stafford	Alliance 29391
Mary Stallings	I Waited for You	Concord Jazz 4620
Dakota Staton	Dakota Staton	Muse 5041
	Spotlight on Dakota Staton	Alliance 31204
Maxine Sullivan	Maxine Sullivan	Audiophile 167
	Uptown	Concord Jazz 4288
Tierney Sutton	Unsung Heroes	Telarc 83477
Teri Thornton	Open Highway	Koch Jazz 8589
Imke Van Oosten	Life Talks	VIA Jazz 9920832
Lydia Van Dam	Tribute to Joni Mitchell	VIA Jazz 9920722
Sarah Vaughan	After Hours	Roulette 93271
	Brazilian Romance	CBS 460156
	Crazy and Mixed Up	Pablo 137
	Gershwin Live	CBS 37277
	How Long Has This Been Going On?	Pablo 821
	One Night Stand: The Town Hall Concert	Blue Note 32139
	Sassy Swings The Tivoli	EmArcy 832 788
	Sarah Vaughan Live in Japan, Vol. 1	Mainstream 701
	Sarah Vaughan Live in Japan, Vol. 2	Mainstream 702
	Sarah Vaughan With Clifford Brown	EmArcy 841 641
	The Benny Carter Sessions	Roulette 28640
Marlene Ver Planck	My Impetuous Heart	DRG 8481
	Sings Alec Wilder	Audiophile 218
Roseanna Vitro	Conviction: Thought of Bill Evans	A 73208
	Passion Dance	Telarc 83385
Dinah Washington	Dinah!	EmArcy 842 139
	First Issue: The Dinah Washington Story	Verve 514 841

FEMALE VOCALISTS (CONTINUED)

ARTIST	TITLE	LABEL & NO.
Michele Weir	Michele Weir With Phil Mattson	Rudy 94
Carla White	Listen Here	Evidence 22109
	The Sweetest Sounds	DIW 422
Weslia Whitfield	My Shining Hour	High Note 7012
Sunny Wilkinson	High Wire	Chartmaker 5020
	Sunny Wilkinson	Positive 78009
Cassandra Wilson	Blue Light 'Til Dawn	Blue Note 81357
	Blue Skies	JMT 834 419
	Days Aweigh	JMT 834 412
	New Moon Daughter	Blue Note 55484
	Traveling Miles	Blue Note 54123
Nancy Wilson	Best of Nancy Wilson	EMI/Capitol 91210
	Lush Life	Blue Note 32745
	Nancy Wilson/Cannonball Adderly	Blue Note 81204
	The Best of Nancy Wilson (Jazz and Blues Sessions)	Capitol Jazz 53921
	The Swingin's Mutual	Blue Note 99190
Norma Winstone	Like Song, Like Weather	Koch Jazz 7875

MALE VOCALISTS

ARTIST	TITLE	LABEL & NO.
Mose Allison	Pure Mose	32 Jazz 32006
	The Mose Chronicles: Live, Vol. 1	Blue Note 29747
Ray Anderson	Wishbone	Grama 79454
Ernie Andrews	No Regrets	Muse 5484
	The Legacy Lives On	Mack Avenue 1003
	*Frankie Capp/Nat Pierce: Juggernaut	Concord Jazz 4040
	*Gene Harris: Live at Town Hall, N.Y.C.	Concord Jazz 4397
Louis Armstrong	Hot Fives and the Hot Sevens, Vol. 3	Columbia 44422
	Jazz Masters 1: Louis Armstrong	Verve 519 818
	Jazz Masters 24: Ella Fitzgerald/ Louis Armstrong	Verve 521 851
	Louis Armstrong Plays W.C. Handy	Columbia 64925
	Priceless Jazz Collection	GRP 9872
Chet Baker	Chet Baker Sings	Capitol 23234
	Let's Get Lost: The Best of Chet Baker Sings	Pacific Jazz 92993
	My Favourite Songs – "The Last Great Concert"	Enja 79600
	My Funny Valentine	Pacific Jazz 28262
	The Best of the Gerry Mulligan Quartet With Chet Baker	Capitol 95481
Marc Beacco	Scampi Fritti	EmArcy 124 062
	The Crocodile Smile	Nova 9143
Tony Bennett	Bennett Sings Ellington Hot & Cool	Columbia 63668
	MTV Unplugged	Columbia 66214
	Perfectly Frank	Columbia 52965
	The Tony Bennett/ Bill Evans Album	Original Jazz Cl. 439
George Benson	Big Boss Band	Warner Bros. 26295
	Tenderly	Warner Bros. 25907
Andy Bey	Andy Bey & The Bey Sisters	Prestige 24245
	Ballads, Blues & Bey	Evidence 22162
	Shades Of Bey	Evidence 22215
Charles Brown	Honey Dripper	Verve 529 848
Cab Calloway	Cab Calloway & Co.	RCA 89560
	Hi-De-Hi-De-Ho	RCA 18524
Mike Campbell	Easy Chair Jazz	Audiophile 272
	Loving Friends	Audiophile 279

MALE VOCALISTS (CONTINUED)

ARTIST	TITLE	LABEL & NO.
Bill Cantos	*Who Are You?*	Pioneer 5158
Vinicius Cantuaria	*Vinicius*	Transparent 500052
Dori Caymmi	*Cinema: A Romantic Vision*	Zebra 44017
Ray Charles	*Best of Ray Charles*	Atlantic 1543
	Ray Charles and Betty Carter/	
	Dedicated to You	Rhino 75259
Freddy Cole	*Merry-Go-Round*	Telarc 83493
	Rio De Janeiro Blue	Telarc 83525
Nat "King" Cole	*Love Is Here to Stay*	Capitol 11355
	Lush Life	Capitol 780595
	Nat King Cole	Capitol 99777
	Nat King Cole Trio 1943/47,	
	The Vocal Sides	LaserLight 15718
	Unforgettable	Capitol 99230
Harry Connick, Jr.	*Come by Me*	Columbia 69618
	Harry Connick, Jr.	Columbia 40702
	To See You	Columbia 68787
	When Harry Met Sally	Columbia 45319
Bing Crosby	*Bing – His Legendary Years*	MCA 10887
	Here Lies Love	Living Era 5043
Sammy Davis, Jr.	*The Sounds of '66*	DCC Jazz 625
Djavan	*Ao Vivo*	Sony 83625
Bob Dorough	*Right on My Way Back Home*	Blue Note 57729
	Too Much Coffee Man	Blue Note 99239
	Who's on First?	Blue Note 23403
Billy Eckstine	*Mr. B and the Band*	Savoy 0264
	Sarah Vaughan and Billy Eckstine: The Irving	
	Berlin Songbook	EmArcy/Polygram 822 526
Kurt Elling	*Close Your Eyes*	Blue Note 30645
	Flirting With Twilight	Blue Note 31113
	Live in Chicago	Blue Note 22211
	The Messenger	Blue Note 52727
	This Time It's Love	Blue Note 93543
Georgie Fame	*Poet in New York*	Go Jazz 6044
Michael Feinstein	*Michael Feinstein Sings Irving Berlin*	Elektra 60744
Michael Franks	*Art of Tea*	Reprise 2230
	Passion Fruit	Warner Bros. 23962
	The Best of Michael Franks:	
	A Backward Glance	Warner Bros. 46855
David Frishberg	*Can't Take You Nowhere*	Fantasy 9651
	Classics	Concord 4462
Gilberto Gil	*Gil & Jorge*	Verve 512 067
	Me, You, Them	Atlantic 83430
João Gilberto	*Amoroso/Brasil*	Warner Archives 45165
	Getz/Gilberto	Verve 810 048
	João	Verve 848 507
	The Legendary João Gilberto	World Pacific 93891
Johnny Hartman	*John Coltrane & Johnny Hartman*	MCA 5661
	Unforgettable	Impulse! 152
Bill Henderson	*Bill Henderson With the*	
	Oscar Peterson Trio	Verve 837 937
	Please Send Me Someone to Love	Collectables 7144
Jon Hendricks	*Boppin at the Blue Note*	Telarc 83320
	Cloudburst	Enja 4032
	Freddie Freeloader	Denon 6302
Maurice Hines	*I've Never Been in Love Before*	ARCD 19240
Al Jarreau	*Breakin' Away*	Warner Bros. 3576
	Live in London	Warner Bros. 25331
Eddie Jefferson	*Come Along With Me*	Original Jazz Cl. 613
	Letter From Home	Original Jazz Cl. 307
	The Jazz Singer	Evidence 22062

MALE VOCALISTS (CONTINUED)

ARTIST	TITLE	LABEL & NO.
Antonio Carlos Jobim	*Antonio Carlos Jobim*	Warner Archives 46114
	Antonio Carlos Jobim and Friends	Verve 531 556
	Quiet Now: Nights of Quiet Stars	Verve 559 733
	Wave	A & M 210 820
Louis Jordan	*Five Guys Named Moe*	Bandstand 1531
Tom Lellis	*Double Entendre*	Beamtide 1012
	Skylark	TMD 2002
	Taken to Heart	Concord Jazz 4574
Ivan Lins	*A Love Affair – The Music of Ivan Lins*	Telarc 83496
	Live At MCG	Heads Up 1005
Kevin Mahogany	*Double Rainbow*	Enja 7097
	Kevin Mahogany	Warner Bros. 46226
	My Romance	Warner Bros. 47025
	Songs and Moments	Enja 8072
	You Got What It Takes	Enja 9039
Bobby McFerrin	*Bang! Zoom*	Blue Note 31677
	Bobby McFerrin	Elektra/Musician 60023
	Bobby McFerrin/Chick Corea –	
	The Mozart Sessions	Sony 62601
	Circle Songs	Sony 62734
	Hush	Sony 48177
	Medicine Music	EMI 92408
	Paper Music	Sony 64600
	Play	Blue Note 95477
	Simple Pleasures	EMI 48059
	Spontaneous Inventions	Blue Note 46298
	The Voice	Elektra/Musician 60366
Jay McShann	*Going to Kansas City*	New World 358
Phil Minton	*Dada Da*	Leo 192
	Songs From A Prison Diary	Leo 196
Mark Murphy	*Beauty And The Beast*	Muse 5355
	Bop For Kerouac	Muse 5253
	Brazil	Muse 5297
	Crazy Rhythm: His Debut Recordings	Decca 670
	I'll Close My Eyes	Muse 5436
	Kerouac Then and Now	Muse 5359
	Night Mood	Milestone 9145
	Rah!	Original Jazz Cl. 141
	Satisfaction Guaranteed	Muse 5215
	Some Time Ago	High Note 7048
	Song for the Geese	RCA Victor 44865
	The Best of Mark Murphy:	
	The Capitol Years	Capitol 33147
	The Dream	Jive 2006
	The Latin Porter	Go Jazz 6051
	The Nat King Cole Songbook	Muse 5308

32 Jazz has released four two-disc sets containing material from Murphy's Muse years: *Jazz Standards* (32063), *Mark Murphy Sings Nat King Cole... and More* (32137), *Songbook* (32105), and *Stolen & Other Moments* (32036). These collections are highly recommended.

Milton Nascimento	*A Arte de Milton*	Verve 829 302
	Crooner	Warner Bros. 47561
	Milton	Verve 543 485
Jackie Paris	*Nobody Else but Me*	Audiophile 245
John Pizzarelli	*Kisses in the Rain*	Telarc 83917
	Let There Be Love	Telarc 83518
	Naturally	Novus 63151
	New Standards	Novus 63172
	Our Love Is Here to Stay	RCA 67501

MALE VOCALISTS (CONTINUED)

ARTIST	TITLE	LABEL & NO.
King Pleasure	*Golden Days*	Original Jazz Cl. 1772
	King Pleasure Sings/	
	Annie Ross Sings	Original Jazz Cl. 217
	Moody's Mood For Love	Blue Note 84463
Baden Powell	*Personalidade (Best of Brazil)*	Verve 514 134
Louis Prima	*Louis Prima Capitol Collectors Series*	Capitol 94072
Kenny Rankin	*Professional Dreamer*	BMG 82124
	The Kenny Rankin Album	Little David 1013
Dennis Rowland	*Now Dig This!*	Concord Jazz 4751
Jimmy Rushing	*Mister Five by Five*	Topaz Jazz 1019
	The You and Me That Used to Be	Bluebird 86460
Jimmy Scott	*All the Way*	Sire 26955
	Over the Rainbow	Milestone 9314
Ian Shaw	*Soho Stories*	Milestone 9316
Frank Sinatra	*Duets*	Capitol 89611
	Francis A. & Edward K. Ellington	Reprise 1024
	Harry James Featuring Frank Sinatra	Columbia 66377
	In the Wee Small Hours	Capitol 96826
	Ol' Blue Eyes Is Back	Reprise 2155
	Sinatra & Jobim	Reprise 46948
	Sinatra at the Sands	Reprise 46947
	Sinatra Sings Select Cole Porter	Capitol 96611
	Sinatra's Swingin' Session	Capitol 94723
	Stardust	Columbia 61703
Curtis Stigers	*Baby Plays Around*	Concord Jazz 4944
Grady Tate	*Body & Soul*	Milestone 9208
Mel Tormé	*16 Most Requested Songs*	Sony 53779
	A & E: An Evening With Mel Tormé	Concord Jazz 4736
	A Vintage Year	Concord Jazz 4341
	At The Red Mill/Live at the Maisonette	Koch Jazz 74
	Great American Songbook	
	Live at Michael's Pub	Telarc 83328
	Lulu's Back in Town	Avenue Jazz 75732
	Mel Tormé and Friends Recorded	
	Live at Marty's	DCC Jazz 631
	Rob McConnell and the Boss Brass	Concord Jazz 4306
	Together Again/For the First Time	Century 592
	Velvet and Brass	Concord Jazz 4667
Caetano Veloso	*Noites Do Norte*	Nonesuch 79631
Joe Williams	*Ballad and Blues Master*	Verve 511 354
	Count Basie Swings — Joe Williams Sings	Verve 519 852
	Here's to Life	Telarc 83357
	Joe Williams With The Mel Lewis	
	Jazz Orchestra	Blue Note 30454
	With the Count Basie Orchestra	Telarc 83329

Music Review and Evaluation Form/Rehearsal Prep Guide

Created By Diana Spradling

1. Title _____

2. Composer/Arranger/Editor _____

3. Publisher _____ Date of Publication _____

   Manuscript/unpublished copy (is it legible?) _____

4. Catalog number _____

5. Voicings and ranges _____

   Key(s) _____ Tempo _____ Age Suitability _____

6. Accompaniment/Instrumental needs _____

   _____

7. Instrumental parts written out   ❏ Yes ❏ No

   Chord changes only: no written out instrumental parts   ❏ Yes ❏ No

   Instrumental and vocal parts separate   ❏ Yes ❏ No

   Instrumental and vocal parts purchased separately   ❏ Yes ❏ No

8. Recorded examples to study

   1. _____

   2. _____

   3. _____

   Other recordings available _____

9. Originally recorded by _____

   Date of recording _____ Place _____

   Recording by arranger's group _____

   Demo recording from publisher _____

10. Chord changes written on vocal parts ❏ Yes ❏ No

11. Length of piece/measures _____

12. Approximate performance time _____

INFORMATION ABOUT THE CHART

Type   ❏ jazz   ❏ pop   ❏ show   ❏ novelty
          ❏ other _____

Style   ❏ blues   ❏ swing   ❏ bossa nova   ❏ samba
         ❏ rock   ❏ other latin ❏ jazz-rock fusion
         ❏ cool   ❏ bebop   ❏ ballad   ❏ funk
         ❏ gospel   ❏ big band   ❏ other _____

Form _____

Historical significance _____

_____

_____

Improvisational opportunities _____

_____

_____

Dance break/choreography opportunities _____

_____

_____

*Videos (**CD ROM/DVD**) to study for style, choreography and performance ideas* _____

_____

_____

Articulations to be taught:

_____

_____

_____

Harmonic devices/complexities:

_____

_____

_____

Rhythmic devices/complexities:

_____

_____

_____

Melodic devices/complexities:

_____

_____

_____

Dramatic devices:

_____

_____

_____

Solo opportunities/requirements:

_____

_____

_____

Potential "problem" spots:

_____

_____

_____

OTHER MUSICAL CONSIDERATIONS

1. Responsibilities of the rhythm section

2. Choice of tempo
   Has the arranger or the publisher adjusted the tempo away from the original intent of the composer?

3. Important musical elements
   Melody, harmony, rhythm, text, style

4. Complexity and construction of harmony
   Who is singing the thirds and sevenths (the most important scale degrees to achieve good intonation in jazz chords)?

5. Appropriateness of the text

6. Space for improvisation
   If there is none allotted, is it possible to create some within the arrangement?

7. Chord changes
   Are they indicated in the vocal score so that guide tones for improvisation can be constructed for less experienced improvisers?

8. Dance relation
   Is the chart connected to or based on a dance which might suggest a certain style or tempo?

9. Extramusical considerations

   Are there any important nonmusical aspects related to the chart?

OTHER INFORMATION/COMMENTS

_____

_____

_____

_____

_____

_____

_____

For the Aspiring Solo Singer

A solo singer needs to commit to a significant amount of time for the research, preparation and practice that precedes the first rehearsal with a rhythm section. The following steps can serve as a guideline for the aspiring solo singer:

1 • *Select songs that you love and that you can technically execute.* A good source for solo literature is the *Great American Songbook,* or the body of songs referred to as "standards" composed by the following: George Gershwin, Richard Rodgers, Duke Ellington and Billy Strayhorn, Jerome Kern, Irving Berlin, Cole Porter, Harold Arlen, Antonio Carlos Jobim and their lyricists. There are many other composers and lyricists who have written wonderful, artistic songs. More recent songwriters include Michel Legrand, Johnny Mandel, Paul Simon, Stevie Wonder, Billy Joel, Lennon and McCartney, Joni Mitchell, Elton John and their lyricists.

2 • *You should be able to understand and perhaps even relate to the text,* and also appreciate and enjoy the melody and harmony of the song. Fake books contain the melody, lyrics and chord changes to tunes and can be an excellent source in the selection process. Realize that the chord changes in a fake book might not be the changes commonly used by jazz musicians. So if possible, find the original version of the song (including the verse) with original chord changes. Match the sophistication of the song to your technical facility and the structure of the song to your musical skill level. Always sing with solid vocal technique.

3 • *Listen to several recordings of the song, both vocal and instrumental.* Locate the original recording as well as the best known ones, and then listen to each recorded example many times. Sing along with each recording, using headphones, until you can imitate what you hear musically. Keep in mind that most of the singers you listen to are older and will have gone through many voice changes. Do not try to reproduce the vocal quality of the recordings; rather, try to imitate phrasing, lyric interpretation, use of vibrato, vocal embellishments and inflections, dramatic devices and elements of contrast. Dissect the recordings: What is the melodic, harmonic and rhythmic treatment? How has the original material been revised, arranged or adjusted? Look for unique characteristics in the recordings that might influence you to draw on your own uniqueness. Prepare study tapes for rhythm section members if the song is not well known.

4 • *Thoroughly learn the song.* Know the complete title, composer, and lyricist. Learn and memorize the chord changes and, if possible, learn to play the chord changes. (This is a requirement for my students). Learn the lyric as poetry, separate from the melody. Learn and be able to play the original melody. Learn the form. Make sure you are singing with pitch accuracy. Tape record your practice sessions and evaluate your progress.

5 • *Decide how the solo will be presented.* Experiment! Practice your song in a variety of keys, styles, and tempos and then determine what makes you most

comfortable. Choose the most appropriate key for your voice and memorize your key. Often the most appropriate key for your voice and range is
not the standard key used by instrumentalists for that song. If, however,
the standard key works well for your voice and the range of the song, it is
to everyone's benefit to perform in the that key. Generally, jazz musicians
tend to favor flat keys (especially horn players), therefore, if you find that
the key of B is the best key for your voice, range and tessitura on a particular song, but B♭ can work equally well, I suggest you select B♭ as your key.
Your jazz accompanists will appreciate your selection! As a pianist, I like to
take pride in my ability to play in any key, but I must admit, I have spent
much more time playing in flat keys. On the other hand, most guitarists,
if pressed, would probably admit a preference for sharp keys; something to
keep in mind if you are being accompanied by solo guitar.

6 • *Choose a mood, style, feel, and/or groove:* medium swing, fast swing, ballad,
shuffle, bossa nova, samba, etc. Choose a tempo and practice at that tempo,
using a metronome. Consider how you will treat the text and whether
or not you might add lyrics of your own to further personalize the song.
Decide on an introduction, how many times you will sing through the
form, whether or not you will scat/improvise, whether or not members of
the rhythm section will solo. Decide how you will end the piece.

7 • *Practice the song until you have mastered, or own, the material.* Most experienced
jazz instrumentalists memorize the melody, form, and chord changes to
hundreds of standard songs. Many times they are capable of playing these
tunes in any key. The singer should not be exempt from this expectation.

8 • Write a lead sheet (see *How to Write Your Own Lead Sheet,* page 110). This
is the road map that will guide the instrumentalists through your arrangement. The more information that you include on the lead sheet, the easier
it will be for the instrumentalists. Make sure your lead sheet is legible and
well marked, including the form and any tempo or key changes. Make one-
sided copies for each member of the rhythm section, and keep the original.
You are now ready to work with the rhythm section!

WORKING WITH THE RHYTHM SECTION

1 • *Call a rehearsal with the rhythm section and be prepared to run the rehearsal.* If
you have done your homework and are musically prepared, this will not
be a difficult process and should be a fun experience. A well-constructed
lead sheet creates a positive, professional work environment. Begin every
rehearsal on time. Specify set up time prior to the rehearsal for instruments and equipment. Be sure the rhythm section knows exactly where the
rehearsal is and how/when they can get their equipment into the space.

2 • *Begin the rhythm section rehearsal by talking the players through the lead sheet*
before running the song. Discuss the key, style, form, tempo, introduction,
number of choruses, improvisation possibilities, and ending. Know how
to count off your song in a manner that will be understood by the players
(bring your metronome). Use hand signals and gestures to conduct changes
and transitions in the arrangement. Know exactly what you would like for

each player to do, and if you do not know exactly how to explain or ask for it, be honest and ask the players for help or suggestions.

3 • *Develop the flexibility to react to and interact with the accompaniment when the music begins.* In order for this to occur, the singer must have practiced enough to thoroughly know the song, and have sufficient ear space to be able to be receptive and responsive to the musical input offered by the rhythm section.

4 • *Make arrangements and provisions for your own equipment and technical needs.* Do not expect the rhythm section to automatically provide it for you. Ideally, you should own your own microphone, amplifier, and monitor speaker. Rehearse on the sound system and know how to EQ the sound. If you are singing on someone else's equipment, be sure that you have sufficient time for a complete sound check and insist that what you request from a sound technician be honored. Your musical and mental comfort level will affect your creativity.

HOW TO WRITE YOUR OWN LEAD SHEET
(created by Sunny Wilkinson)

The purpose of your chart is to give the instrumental accompanists as much information as possible, as quickly as possible.

Before you put pencil to paper, you need to know the following:

1. In order to make copies easily, use a dark, soft lead pencil or black ink on 8 by 10-inch staff paper with margins. Make sure you buy staff paper that has no more than 10 staves per page, as you will need extra space for lyrics and/or instructions. Also, there are several music writing software programs that include lead sheet templates

2 • Before you begin your chart, determine the form of your song. This will help in the advance planning and the physical layout and appearance of your lead sheet.

3 • Determine the best key for your vocal range. If your key differs from the sheet music or your original source, you will need to transpose the chord changes.

4 • Make sure you are consistent, accurate and exact in your transposition.

5 • Use double bars at the end of each phrase (usually every eight measures) and at the beginning of each new phrase. These are marked with rehearsal letters in the margin and will usually follow your song form.

6 • Instructions are written above or below the staff (usually below, as the chord symbols will occupy most of the space above the staff), and use brackets that indicate to which staff the instructions belong.

7 • With the possible exception of the final line of music, each line of staff paper should have a full line of music. Fill in each staff from the left edge to the right.

8 • Take great care when copying your chord symbols. Make them legible and large enough to read from a distance. If the chord symbol on your source (perhaps the original sheet music) says "Cmaj7," copy it exactly. (C7 is a different chord!)

9 • Below is an example of a basic chord chart with diagonal slashes to indicate the beats in a bar. Usually, you will write four measures per staff, as follows:

EXAMPLE AP3.1

You have three methods available to help you return to a previous section of the music. The first method is the repeat sign. Repeat signs generally work in pairs, with the music between the left and right signs repeated once, unless otherwise notated.

EXAMPLE AP3.2

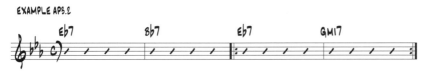

If there is no repeat sign on the left side of the staff, then the music is repeated from the beginning of the chart.

EXAMPLE AP3.3

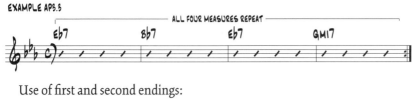

Use of first and second endings:

EXAMPLE AP3.4

The second method is *D.S. al Coda,* an Italian phrase that means, "go to the sign and then go to the coda." This is a very literal instruction. When a player sees *D.S. al Coda,* they will look back into the chart until they find the sign, and begin reading the chart again from that spot. When the player reaches the *to Coda* symbol (⊕), they will locate the coda sign and continue reading the chart.

EXAMPLE AP3.5

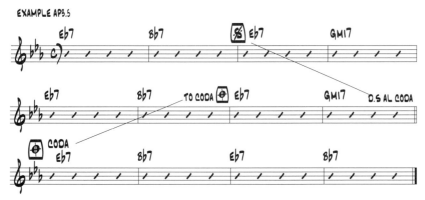

The third method is *D.C.*, which is an abbreviation for the Italian phrase "da capo," which means "to the head." When the player sees this symbol, they return to the very beginning of the piece.

Now you are ready to put pencil to paper! Most lead sheets are written in one of two ways:

- *Using two staves*. Write the melody on the top staff, the chord changes (using symbols) on the bottom staff, and the lyrics between the two staves.

- *Using one staff*. Write the melody (or slashes representing the rhythms of the melody) on the staff, the chord changes above the staff, and the lyrics below the staff.

1 • Write the title of the song at the top of the page (above the first staff) with the name of the composer, lyricist and arranger (if appropriate) to the right of the title.

2 • On the first staff write the clef, key signature and time signature. Include the key signature on every stave and follow it with a bracket in order to avoid confusion about the use of accidentals. Remember to be neat. Above the first staff write the "feel" of the song (ballad, swing, latin, etc.) and the word "Intro" in brackets to give the player the added information they will need. Next write a four or eight measure introduction (if you have "arranged" one) on the top stave. If you have arranged an eight bar intro-duction which has the same chord changes in each four bar phrase, you may use a repeat sign (see example AP3.3 on page 111). If it is a four bar introduc-tion, put a double bar after the fourth measure. Generally you should plan on writing three to four measures per stave, depending on the number of words in the lyrics or the number of chord changes. Use a ruler to draw bar lines and make sure they are perpendicular to the staff lines.

3 • You are now at the main part of your chart. What follows are three exam-ples of song forms (12-bar blues, **AABA**, **ABAC**) that you may use as guides for your lead sheet. Notice that in all of the examples the sections of the song (usually notated with rehearsal letters) occur at the beginnings and endings of the staff. This method of writing makes it much easier for the players to read and follow. Also, notice that the chord symbols line up with the appropriate beats in the measure. You should also include the original melody (with guide lyrics), which is another source of information that can help instrumentalists follow the chart.

DOCTOR BLUES

EXAMPLE AP3.6

GOT RHYTHM?

EXAMPLE AP3.7 (AABA)

BUT BEAUTIFUL

Music by JIMMY VAN HEUSEN
Words by JOHNNY BURKE
Arranged by STEVE ZEGREE

Finally, one of the most important characteristics that will help ensure the success of the solo singer (or any musician) has nothing to do with music. I am referring to personal responsibility, attitude, and professionalism.

The personal skills and characteristics a soloist should develop include:

- *Punctuality.* If you are five minutes early, you are ten minutes late. Allow yourself sufficient time to arrive comfortably in advance of all rehearsals and performances.

- *Preparation and organization.* Know your material. Have it readily accessible. Have a pencil.

- *Professionalism.* Be pleasant. Be courteous and appreciative. Remember to acknowledge, recognize and thank your accompanists. They are *not* in fact "accompanists," but more accurately "essential collaborative musicians."

- *Cooperation.* Be sensitive to the other musicians. Be open to suggestions and be flexible enough to make adjustments if necessary. There is very little tolerance for **DWA**s(Divas With Attitude… this is *not* gender specific!)

- *Personality.* Remember that a performance may last (in real time) anywhere from five minutes to two hours. The remainder of your time together with your collaborative musicians is *more* important than the time on stage. What is your personality? What is your mood? Do you laugh easily? Heard any good jokes lately? It is important to be a person that other people want to be around, and, more importantly, will recommend to others for future gigs. If you cannot say something positive when discussing another person, do not say anything. As a rule, when speaking of others (when they are not present), you should be willing to say the same thing if they were in your immediate presence.

A reputation is built on attitudes and perceptions, musical and personal. On a personal level, you have only one opportunity to create an initial impression. Make the most of that opportunity! One may earn a reputation as the best singer in town, and then come the "buts":

- but she is never on time

- but she has such an ego

- but she treats everyone like second-class citizens

No one wants or needs any "buts" associated with their name. Musicians will invariably want to associate with the *second* best singer in town if they have the best attitude and no "buts."

References

─────────── BOOKS ───────────

JAZZ

TITLE	WEBSITE
Advance Music Maieracker Strasse 18 D-72108 Rottenburg/Neckar Germany	www,advancemusic.com
♦ *Jamey Aebersold Jazz* (perhaps the most comprehensive single source for materials relating to jazz) PO Box 1244 New Albany, IN 47171-1244 (800) 456-1388	www.jazzbooks.com
The New Grove Dictionary of Jazz, 2nd edition	www.grovemusic.com
Sher Music Company PO Box 445 Petaluma, CA 94953 (800) 444-7437	www.shermusic.com

JAZZ VOICE OR VOCAL GROUPS

TITLE	AUTHOR	PUBLISHER
American Singing Groups: A History 1940-1990	Jay Warner	Billboard
Easy To Remember: The Great American Songwriters and their Songs	William Zinsser	???
Harmony Vocals	Mike Campbell and Tracee Lewis	M.I. Press
Jazz and Show Choir Handbook II	Doug Anderson	Hinshaw Music
Jazz Singing	Will Friedwald	Collier Books
Professional Singer's Handbook	Gloria Rusch	Hal Leonard
Sing Your Story: The Art of Jazz Singing	Jay Clayton	Advance Music
Swingle Singing	Ward Swingle	Shawnee Press

JAZZ HISTORY TEXTBOOKS

TITLE	AUTHOR	PUBLISHER
Jazz 101: A Complete Guide to Learning and Loving Jazz	John Szwed	Hyperion
Jazz: A History	Frank Tirro	W.W. Norton & Co.
JazzStyles: History and Analysis	Mark C. Gridley	Prentice Hall
Visions of Jazz: The First Century	Gary Giddins	Oxford University Press

JAZZ THEORY TEXTBOOKS

TITLE	AUTHOR	PUBLISHER
The Jazz Piano Book	Mark Levine	Sher Music
The Jazz Theory Book	Mark Levine	Sher Music
Jazz Theory and Practice	Richard Lawn and Jeffrey Helmer	Wadsworth

VOCAL IMPROVISATION BOOKS

TITLE	AUTHOR	PUBLISHER
Effortless Mastery	Kenny Werner	Jamey Aebersold
Guide for Jazz and Scat Vocalists	Dennis Di Blasio	Jamey Aebersold
Jazz Conception Series (vocal version)	Jim Snidero	Jamey Aebersold
♦ *A New Approach, Vol. 21*	Jamey Aebersold	Jamey Aebersold
SCAT! Vocal Improv Techniques	Bob Stoloff	Jamey Aebersold
♦ *Vocal Improvisation*	Michele Weir	Advance Music
Vocal Improvisation: An Instrumental Approach	Patty Coker and David Baker	

PUBLICATIONS

MAGAZINES AND PERIODICALS

TITLE	WEBSITE
Down Beat	www.downbeat.com

102 N. Haven Road
Elmhurst, IL 60126-2970
(630) 941-3210

Jazz Educators Journal . . . . www.iaje.org
  P.O. Box 724
  Manhattan, KS 66505

Jazz Improv Magazine . . . . www.jazzimprov.com
  PO Box 57
  Grafton, VT 05146-0057

Jazz Times . . . . www.jazztimes.com
  8737 Colesville Rd.
  Silver Spring, MD 20910-3921

Jazziz . . . . www.jazziz.com
  2650 North Military Trail
  Fountain Square 11, Suite 140
  Boca Raton, FL 33431
  (561) 893-6867

Schwann Inside Jazz and Classical . . . . www.schwann.com
  1289 Santa Anita Court
  Woodland, CA 95776
  (530) 669-5077

WEBSITES

TITLE	WEBSITE
American Popular Soing	www.americanpopularsong.com
Fred Waring's America	www.libraries.psu.edu/crsweb/specol/waring

  Pennsylvania State University
  313 Pattee Library
  University Park, PA 16802
  (814) 863-2911

The Jazz Channel . . . . www.betonjazz.com

Jazz Corner.com . . . . www.jazzcorner.com

Jazz Singers.com . . . . www.jazzsingers.com

The Jazz Store . . . . www.thejazzstore.com
  212 Glenridge Ave.
  Montclair, NJ 07042
  (800) 558-9513

The Vocal Jazz Resource . . . . www.jazzvocal.com

PROFESSIONAL ORGANIZATONS

ORGANIZATION	WEBSITE
American Choral Directors Association (ACDA) . . .	www.acdaonline.org/

  502 SW 38th Street
  Lawton Oklahoma 73505
  (580) 355-8161

International Association
  for Jazz Education (IAJE) . . . . www.iaje.org
  PO Box 724
  Manhattan, KS
  (785) 776-8744

ORGANIZATION	WEBSITE
International Federation for Choral Music (IFCM)	www.choralnet.org/ifcm/index.shtml

Music Educators National Conference (MENC) ... www.menc.org
1806 Robert Fulton Drive
Reston, VA 20191-4348
(703) 860-4000

RECORDING SOURCES

ORGANIZATION	WEBSITE
Amazon.com	www.amazon.com
DJ Records (Doug Anderson)	www.dj-records.com
Maine-ly a cappella	www.a-cappella.com

PO Box 159
Southwest Harbor, ME 04679

The Music Resource .... www.themusicresource.com

Primarily A Cappella .... www.singers.com
862 Sir Francis Drake Blvd. #185
San Anselmo, CA 94960

RECORDING CREDITS

Produced by Steve Zegree and Blair Bielawski

Recording, mixing, mastering .... Western Sound Studios
John Campos, Director
School of Music
Western Michigan University
Kalamazoo, MI 49008

Nexus Studios
Pat Lilley
Waukesha, WI 53186

Engineers .... John Campos
Jed Scott
Rachael Flanigan
Seth Ashby

Assistant Engineer .... Ryan Billington

Mixed by .... Steve Zegree
Jed Scott
Rachael Flanigan
Ryan Billington
Seth Ashby

Performers .... All group vocals performed by Gold Company
But Beautiful phrasing examples • Sunny Wilkinson

Arrangers .... *But Beautiful* • Van Heusen/Burke
arranged by Steve Zegree .... Shawnee Press

Doctor Blues • Peter Blair .... Heritage Music Press

This Masquerade • Russell
arranged by Steve Zegree .... Shawnee Press

One in a Million • Peter Blair ... Heritage Music Press

VOCAL JAZZ PUBLISHERS

(octavos, fake books, and other books on the subject of jazz)

PUBLISHER   WEBSITE

Hal Leonard Corporation . . . . www.halleonard.com
    7777 W. Bluemound Rd.
    Milwaukee, Wl 53213
    (414)774-3630

Heritage Jazz Works . . . . www.lorenz.com
    Heritage Music Press
    PO Box 802
    Dayton, OH 45401-0802
    (800) 444-1144

Scott Music Publications . . . . http://scottmusic.com/
    PO Box 598
    Lynnwood, WA 98046

Shawnee Press . . . . www.shawneepress.com
    49 Waring Drive
    Delaware Water Gap, PA 18327
    (800) 962-8584

University of Northern Colorado Press . . . . www.jazzpress@arts.unco.edu/uncjazz
    Department of Music
    University of Northern Colorado
    Greeley, CO 80639

Warner Brothers Publications . . . . www.warnerbrospublications.com
    15800 N.W. 48th Ave.
    Miami, FL 33014
    (305) 620-1500